Arriving Late

of related interest

Spectrum Women
Walking to the Beat of Autism
Foreword by Lisa Morgan
Edited by Michelle Garnett and Barb Cook
ISBN 978 1 78592 434 7
eISBN 978 1 78450 806 7

Camouflage
The Hidden Lives of Autistic Women
Sarah Bargiela
Illustrated by Sophie Standing
ISBN 978 1 78592 566 5
eISBN 978 1 78592 667 9

Women and Girls with Autism Spectrum Disorder
Understanding Life Experiences from Early Childhood to Old Age
Sarah Hendrickx
Foreword by Judith Gould
ISBN 978 1 84905 547 5
eISBN 978 0 85700 982 1

ARRIVING LATE

The lived experience of women
receiving a late autism diagnosis

Jodi Lamanna

Jessica Kingsley Publishers
London and Philadelphia

First published in Great Britain in 2024 by Jessica Kingsley Publishers
An imprint of John Murray Press

3

Copyright © Jodi Lamanna 2024

A CIP catalogue record for this title is available from the British Library
and the Library of Congress

ISBN 978 1 83997 510 3
eISBN 978 1 83997 511 0

Printed and bound by CPI Group (UK) Ltd, Croydon, CR0 4YY

Jessica Kingsley Publishers' policy is to use papers that are natural,
renewable and recyclable products and made from wood grown in
sustainable forests. The logging and manufacturing processes are expected
to conform to the environmental regulations of the country of origin.

Jessica Kingsley Publishers
Carmelite House
50 Victoria Embankment
London EC4Y 0DZ

www.jkp.com

John Murray Press
Part of Hodder & Stoughton Ltd
An Hachette Company

Contents

Glossary

These terms and their definitions are to be used as a guide and a starting point for understanding autism and its related language. They do not provide a comprehensive definition or analysis of the term.

Ableist
Attitudes by non-disabled people where disability is viewed in a deficit form, usually accompanied by prejudice and discrimination

Allistic
Not autistic

Asperger's
Now incorporated under the umbrella term "autism"

Autism
Differences in social communication and patterns of interest

Autistic burnout
Life stressors[1] outweigh the resources to deal with the stress, leading to chronic exhaustion and loss of ability

Hyperlexia
Significantly advanced[2] reading level for age

Masking or camouflaging
Covering up the traits of autism to pass as non-autistic

Neurodivergent
An umbrella[3] term for people who are autistic, ADHD and other unique brain types

Neurotypical
Not autistic

Sensory overwhelm[4]
Too much sensory input, resulting in an inability to cope

Stim
Self-stimulatory behaviour[5] leading to self-regulation

Twice exceptional
Both gifted[6] (outstanding potential) and with disability

Acknowledgements

I would like to acknowledge the Traditional Custodians of the land where this book was written. I pay my respects to their Elders past, present and emerging.

Thank you to each person who shared their story for this book. Your words, your insight and your lived experience make this such a rich narrative. It is my hope that by sharing your stories others may find connection and understanding in their own journey. Thank you for trusting me with your story.

Also, thank you to my family who have supported me in writing this book and in exploring my own late diagnosis of autism. A special thanks to my daughter who provided feedback on the draft chapters.

And thank you to the team at Jessica Kingsley Publishers who saw the value of shared stories.

Content warning

Some of the stories make reference to homelessness, bullying, suicide and other issues that may potentially be triggering. If you find yourself adversely affected by the contents of the stories, please reach out and connect with your local support service.

Preface

Stories are important because they draw us together, create community and foster a sense of belonging. The stories within this book tell of the journey to late autism diagnosis: stories of discovery, strength, self-awareness and belonging. The stories are shared by late-diagnosed autistic females* who convey their lived experience of autism. The stories showcase personalities, strengths and struggles. The willingness of the participants in sharing their stories demonstrates their generosity as well as their passion for creating an enhanced understanding of the breadth of the autistic spectrum. I am deeply grateful to each person for sharing their story.

My hope is that you, as the reader, will see part of your story reflected within this book, or that it may

---

* For this book, female refers to cisgender female, non-binary and/or identifying as female.

bring a greater understanding and awareness of someone in your world who is reflected in these stories. So, get comfortable and engage in these stories as a friend and ally. May the words of these stories change the way you see autism, and yourself.

CHAPTER 1

All journeys have a beginning

A JOURNEY INVOLVES MOVEMENT and rest. There may be missteps, faltering, doubts and pain, but there is also often purpose, determination and pure joy. In this book, there is a collection of lived experience stories about the journey to late autism diagnosis. The storytellers share the way forward for them and what they discovered on the journey. You are invited to share in their journeys in the pages that follow. By sharing these journeys, it is hoped that their stories will light the way forward in your journey and for those around you.

In this chapter, and in part of the *Talking about the stories* chapter (Chapter 9), I will make use of references from research literature to support some of the things that I will be writing about. I promise you that I will not do this continually throughout the book as I want the voices of the participants to stand out – their voices to be our friend as they tell their story. The reason I do use some references in this chapter and in Chapter 9 is that I have a background in academic research, and as a reader and researcher, it helps me to know that the claims or statements being made about autism are in fact true or have been backed up by research. If this style of writing doesn't appeal to you, please start at Chapter 2 and read about Julian and her journey to late diagnosis of autism. The story is sure to draw you in!

Why write about the journey to autism diagnosis?

Up until I was 45 years of age, my recurring thought was "I don't fit". I don't hold down long-term jobs like others can: I have anxiety attacks three months into a mundane, boring job and then I have to quit. I have out-of-the-box ideas where I can see how ideas can come to fruition, but these ideas are seen to be unconventional and unacceptable by others.

And, increasingly, my oddities – such as an inability to go into a supermarket without becoming panic-stricken from sensory overwhelm, or my food aversions and intolerances – seemed to intensify as the years progressed. I couldn't fit into the mould that others so effortlessly seemed to fit in. It seemed that "normal" was not attainable. At times, that feeling of difference led to a sense of isolation and frustration with myself. My thought was that I just need to try harder, that it was my fault for not being what I thought I needed to be.

When I finally decided to investigate autism, it described many facets of myself. At the same time, it didn't. I didn't twirl, and I didn't line up my toys (or my bespoke stationery items). I was able to maintain eye contact and hold conversations. And I had empathy – which I thought ruled out autism for me. Yet, as I searched for community, the amazing stories of #*actuallyautistic* folk on social media reflected my own stories, struggles and experiences. There was hope that maybe I did fit somewhere. That maybe there was a community where I belonged.

However, I kept striving, trying to fit in a neurotypical world, not taking into account my own needs and limitations. When my autism diagnosis came, I was burnt out, but the diagnosis gave me permission and a framework to accept myself for who I am. There was freedom and a lightness in that space – and an unleashing of my suppressed quirks!

After my diagnosis, it became apparent in my quest for further knowledge about autism and myself that many others had a similar journey to late diagnosis. I read that males were more likely to be diagnosed with autism than females,[7] and the literature cited the difficulties in gaining a diagnosis for females due to differences in male and female presentation of autism.[8] Likewise, there were difficulties for adult females accessing an autism assessment due to the cost of an assessment, along with the long wait times and lack of understanding about diagnosing autism in adulthood.[9] These experiences are not limited to the female population, but it did appear to be more concentrated with this cohort. That's when I decided that the stories of late-diagnosed autistic females needed to be shared to help create awareness of the lived experience, and to create community where other late-diagnosed females know that they have found their home.

Focusing on female participants was an intentional decision, not designed to be exclusionary or discriminatory toward others, but as a recognition of the unique challenges that female autistic people experience in the journey to diagnosis. First, as mentioned earlier, this is because autism is identified in males at a higher rate than for females.[10] The ratios vary, depending on the research study and on the sample used for the research. The reasons for this diagnosis bias have not been fully determined.[11]

Second, there has been limited literature on the experiences of females with autism,[12] and with autistic adults in general.[13] This is changing with more first-person books coming out about the experiences of autism (some of which are listed in the resources section at the end of this book) and a recognition that this is an under-researched area in the research literature.

A third factor in focusing on females was the potential for misdiagnosis in females leading to a late diagnosis of autism.[14] Autism has been linked to anxiety, depression and other conditions, and these conditions can overshadow autism, leading to misdiagnosis and late diagnosis.[15] It is worth noting that the changing definitions and diagnostic criteria of autism can help explain the growing number of diagnoses of autism in later life.[16] Similarly, detecting autism in individuals without language or intellectual delay with traditional diagnostic tools can mean that diagnoses may be missed.[17]

For the participants in this book, a general lack of understanding about the breadth of the spectrum contributed to their own late diagnosis. It has only been in recent years that a greater awareness of autism is emerging,[18] especially in what it looks like in females. Receiving a late autism diagnosis impacts the individual as they have lost the opportunity for early support and intervention, and this can affect the mental health and overall wellbeing of females.[19]

Similarly, there is some question as to whether there is a female presentation of autism.[20] As yet, this is inconclusive, but it is noted that autism assessment tools have been developed with a male sample.[21] There is a call for assessment tools to be less gendered so that all genders are reflected in the assessment tool.[22] Likewise, it has been recognised that females may be more likely to mask or camouflage their autistic traits in an effort to fit in with their peers, which may hinder a timely diagnosis.[23] Masking – or camouflaging – autistic traits has received research attention in recent years[24] and is also well documented in first-person experiences which will be explored further in this book.

Sharing stories about autism is important because it highlights the broad spectrum of autism, not just a narrow representation. With this in mind, the stories in this book are intended to show how autism can present in a variety of ways. It is hoped that this representation can then translate to awareness in the greater community and those on the spectrum can come to a place of understanding and acceptance of their own way of being. The stories of the participants and those from other literature show that many personal struggles and differences in individuals can be explained and accepted through the late diagnosis of autism.

Diagnosis

For this book, only participants with formal diagnoses have been included; however, it is important to note that autistic self-diagnosis needs to be taken into consideration. Formal diagnosis may not be accessible to all of the autistic population, but access to information – such as finding out about autistic traits – can be more readily available. Lack of accessibility to a formal assessment can be attributed to the time and financial cost of an assessment, and physical accessibility if the individual is in a rural or remote geographical area. Additionally, for some individuals, sharing their life story with a stranger can be an overwhelming and anxiety-provoking experience that is a barrier to assessment.[25]

For this book, seven participants were chosen to provide a broad range of lived experience. Participants ranged in age from their late 20s to early 70s. Some were in committed relationships and some were single; some were parents, some were not; and they had diverse careers. For the purpose of this book, late diagnosis was aged 25 and over. This age was chosen so that there would be no confusion about the participant being beyond childhood when diagnosed. The participants will be introduced at the beginning of their own chapter, but an overview of the participants can be found in Table 1.1.

The call for participants was intentionally international, although due to the linguistic limitations of the author, participants told their story in English. The aim of the stories was to provide broad and diverse lived experience so that readers could see themselves, or someone they know, in the stories. This was important because autism can historically be viewed as a narrow stereotype, whereas autistic people can have any variation of intelligence, interests, creativity, verbal ability and social capability. It is important that this cross-section is shown so that diagnosis – and the key to understanding oneself – can be given where autism was previously unrecognised.

Table 1.1: Demographics of participants

Pseudonym	Age at diagnosis	Country of residence
Julian	44	UK
Matilda	38	UK
Rebecca	32	Australia
Sydney	45	UK
Zoë	44	Canada
Elizabeth	70	Australia
Rose	58	UK

Why the narrative method?

This book uses the narrative method – telling stories – where stories are collected from individuals about their lived and told experiences. John Creswell, a qualitative research expert,[26] wrote that narrative stories define identities and perceptions of self. For this book, to shed light on the identities of individuals, participants were interviewed over two or three sessions, and those interviews were recorded and then transcribed. The participants were provided with their individual interview transcripts and were given the opportunity to check them for accuracy. This ensured that the stories that were told were viewed as accurate by the participant and the interviewer. The chapters were then created from the interview transcripts; they are the participants' own words that have been edited for clarity and sequence. It should be noted that some sections of their story appear for the first time in the *Talking about the stories* chapter or in the concluding chapter. Sharing stories can unlock memories, create connection between the storyteller and listener, and can highlight universal themes. Some words that may have mixed meanings have been included in the chapters as they reflect the participants' own views. For example, Matilda in Chapter 3 speaks of the mad community.

This wording is retained as it reflects a movement where people with disability are claiming back terms from ableist spaces. Using a narrative method – that is, having autistic individuals tell their story – allows key messages to be heard. The participants were able to share what they deemed to be important.

Similarly, it has been noted that autistic people often feel excluded from research.[27] By featuring autistic voices, the lived experience and diversity of autism can be shared. It is important to demonstrate a breadth of stories that reflect what the experiences are like for autistic women. To see oneself reflected in the stories can help to bring a sense of validation, connection and acceptance of identity.

Overview of the following chapters

The following chapters in the book allow each participant to share their story of their journey to late autism diagnosis. A brief outline of their chapter is shown as follows.

Julian reflects on her childhood and instances of bullying and isolation, and how post-diagnosis she found meaningful friendships and shared interests. Julian also provides strategies that help her to manage employment.

Matilda speaks of her advocacy in the autistic and

mental health space, and how she manages her own health through strategies and support from family. Her love of studying is linked with her special interests, and in her working life she educates others about autism and mental health.

Rebecca articulates her understanding of autism and the benefits of understanding herself through the lens of autism. Rebecca's special interests as a psychologist include trauma, chronic pain and illness, and sleep.

Sydney tells of her social struggles, her escape into the woods and her experience with burnout. Sydney's story highlights the misunderstandings that can occur between autistic people and neurotypical people, and the joy that comes from finding people who understand her.

At the time of telling their story, Zoë was experiencing burnout from a challenging employment situation, and their marriage was ending. S'he tells of their journey to diagnosis and how the outcome was not as s'he expected or hoped.

Elizabeth was in her 70s when she told her story. Her insights reflect a life lived in a country town where autism was not recognised or understood. Elizabeth has experienced traumatic life circumstances and mental health challenges, and she describes her life in colourful colloquialisms.

Rose shares how autism has had an impact on her working life, and she reflects on what life was like growing up as an undiagnosed autistic person. Post-diagnosis, Rose reframed life events in a way that creates personal sense and meaning.

The *Talking about the stories* chapter takes the themes from the stories told by the participants and discusses them further. Examining themes from the stories of lived experience is important as it can illuminate areas that need additional support, and it shows the strengths of the participants which reflects the strengths in us as readers who have our own journeys, whether we be neurodivergent or neurotypical. The style of this chapter is more academic with subheadings and references from academic literature.

The last chapter finishes with final comments from the participants and a list of resources that have been recommended by the participants and the author. These resources are not exhaustive and are not to be seen as endorsed by the author and the participants; however, they provide a range of advice, support and insight into the lived experience of autism.

Before we commence with everyone's stories, I'd like to share my story to set the scene around my journey to late diagnosis of autism, and what it has looked like from the other side of diagnosis.

My story

As a child, I was imaginative, reserved at times, and my repetitive behaviours weren't obvious. For example, as a small child, I would suck my thumb as a way of self-soothing. This continued until I was ten years old – much older than many children – but it was a subtle stim. Other repetitive behaviours were in my imagination where I would create worlds of animals that I would look after and that needed feeding every day. I also played musical instruments, an activity where repetition is encouraged. Playing musical scales to warm up was very soothing. I have been told that as a small child I would have tantrums that now could be interpreted as a response to sensory overload. Again, these things weren't recognised when I was a child, and it is not surprising as there wasn't an awareness that these were autistic traits back then.

Socially, as a child, I didn't feel too different from my peers. I had good friends and I moved from school to school enough to learn how to navigate new social situations. As an adult, and a little more aware of myself, I felt that I didn't fit. I would try to do "normal" jobs, and manage socially, but there were times when I was so upset with myself as I didn't fit: I couldn't do things the way that others could, especially with work.

Cognitively, I could do the work fine, but if it was a boring job, I would only last three months and then need to move on. Looking back, I realised that I needed an intellectual challenge and a purpose. Fortunately, with additional education, later jobs were more interesting and stimulating.

As an adult, I found joy in studying. I love to learn new things, and the pattern and predictability of studying suited me – although that probably wasn't obvious when I was a teenager! In a course of study in education and teaching, I learned more about special needs in the classroom (that's their label, not mine). This included autism. And as I did, I read memoirs and other books about autism so that I could understand, and be aware of, the experiences of others.

In recent years, and with further study, I became more aware that autism can look different from the stereotypes. On forums, autistic people were explaining how they were creative, imaginative, had empathy and could often manage in social situations. It became clear to me that even if I wasn't autistic, a lot of these traits mirrored my own. And their sensitivities aligned with mine. Even if I didn't belong to their group, I knew that there were others like me. That brought a sense of relief. At the time, though, I didn't feel the need to explore the connection with autism further as I was able to manage my environment and my work, and things were going well.

It was only when I was working in a role where there was sensory overload every day – noise, smells, movement, lights – with no rest or breaks in between, that I finally realised I was not coping. It took me a while to reach this realisation – months after I had started to lose speech and functioning memory. That's because I often don't realise what I'm feeling. I've read that this is called alexithymia, and it accurately describes why I don't know what my body is telling me. I'm pretty clueless when it comes to knowing that I'm not doing okay. Except now, as I'm growing older, I've had enough experience to recognise some of the signs. I know now that if I can't use words to express myself, then I'm overloaded. I also know that if I'm rocking, scratching my skin or flapping my hands, I'm likely to be distressed.

Even though I began to realise that I wasn't coping in my work role in the high-sensory situation, I didn't want to give up my job. I didn't want it to be like so many other jobs I've had where I only coped for a short amount of time before having anxiety attacks and not being able to return to work. So I did everything I could to hold on to my job. I saw counsellors, I went for walks, I worked with yarn, I read a book. And then I decided to have an autism assessment because I reasoned that there would be recommendations in the report that could help me get accommodations at work, such as a quiet room to sit in. I thought that then, maybe, there would be a way that I could work in an environment that was not built for me.

The diagnosis came after I could no longer go to work due to excessive anxiety which was linked to the sensory overwhelm at work. It had been a good job, one that I loved, and the people were fantastic. But I was also broken by it. I left the job feeling ashamed that I couldn't manage it when everyone else could.

From there, I began to accept that I'd probably need to work from home in an environment that I could control. With my pets and my people. That was hard to accept as there were so many things that I wanted to do and many of those jobs were not possible without being in an office. The Covid-19 pandemic helped change things a bit by normalising working from home, but it is still not easy to convince many employers that working from home is the best option.

Knowing that I am autistic helps me, though. It allows me to use the tools I need to manage situations. For example, if I'm going into a busy place such as the shops, I'll use my noise-filtering ear plugs. And I might take a small, plush toy to hold in my pocket if needed (it really seems to help). And a socially accepted stim (repetitive and soothing behaviour) is crochet. I can take some yarn and a crochet hook with me, and it helps to calm and centre me. Knitting does, too. After doing a row or two of knitting, I can feel the core of my body relax, and my breathing calms down. I also use tools such as a weighted blanket and have fabrics that are beautifully tactile. Before, I would have just powered on until I had to hibernate for a few days to recover. Now, I can use things such as a weighted blanket or a soft toy to help myself regulate again. Sounds childish, but again it's recognising the validity of my needs. I'm wired differently. Before, I thought I should be able to cope in challenging sensory situations. Now, I know that I can do some things, but only for a certain amount of time before I need to retreat and recharge. And that's okay.

I still struggle, though. I'd like to be able to do what "everybody else" does. I'm trying to be kinder and more accepting of myself. I'm doing okay with that. But there is part of me that just wishes I could fit in, even when I think that might be a bit boring.

I have kept my autism diagnosis mostly to myself, sharing it only with family and a small number of friends. I also shared it with a couple of people at my work before I left as I wanted them to understand what I was going through and how hard I was trying.

Aside from the autism diagnosis helping me to

accept my traits and my disposition, there are many times where I don't believe that I am actually autistic. This is exacerbated when autism is portrayed as being socially insensitive, emotionally unavailable and being gifted in IT or maths (maths is not a strength for me!).

Knowing about my autism diagnosis wouldn't have been helpful when I was younger as it's only now that people are realising that the autism spectrum is broad and rich and deep. There was, and still is, limited understanding about what autism is. Because the stereotypes of autism are still the main understanding of autism for many people, it doesn't seem helpful to share that I have an autism diagnosis. Plus, I'm exceptional at masking and can do well in social situations – until I'm overwhelmed by the noise, lights, movement and the social effort. That is, I can do social situations well for short amounts of time before I need to come home and sit quietly for a while.

It would appear that I mask a lot. I'm not aware of it, but then I'm not aware of a lot of what I'm feeling, or even sometimes thinking. But I do know how to initiate conversations and make people feel at ease. This has been a learned thing, though. Since the diagnosis, I've unmasked a bit by telling people close to me if I'm not coping at the time (it's not usually obvious to others), or if I need the lights less bright, or if I need silence so that I can recover from a situation that had too much sensory input.

When I need to share about my diagnosis, I'll be specific about an aspect, not the whole diagnosis. For example, in one of my work roles, I specified that I needed to work from home because of sensory sensitivities. This was taken well by the employer. They were willing to accommodate my need to work from home. They also knew that I would work hard and do the work.

If I don't look after myself, I'm likely to experience burnout. This has happened a bit. The most recent was during the time when I was having the autism assessment. The burnout led to a loss of speech and forgetting words such as "fridge". I'd do more pointing and hand-waving to explain things.

Autistic burnout for me also meant that I had a significantly reduced capacity to be around people. I couldn't manage to spend time with people outside of my immediate family because it was all too overwhelming. Even people moving near me was too much. Food sensitivities increased with burnout, too. At one stage, I was just eating toast, cereal and boiled eggs. Anything else was just too much.

Thankfully, recognising burnout, and the sensory

factors contributing to it, has allowed me to adjust my workload and my work environment, and give myself a little grace to allow time to heal.

CHAPTER 2

A right to know

Julian

England · Diagnosed autistic at age 44
Julian and her wife have been together since the year 2000, long before they found out that they were both autistic. They like to visit the lesbian hotspots of the UK: Brighton, Halifax and Hebden Bridge.

I LIVE IN THE UK with my wife, Alex, and we are both late-diagnosed autistic. My family are probably autistic. My dad definitely is. He agrees that he is, although he doesn't have a formal diagnosis because he doesn't need one in his 70s. I'm thinking more and more that my mum probably is as well but in a different kind of way. And my sister is quite similar to my mum, so there's the four of us in our family and I think probably we all are.

I work as a piano teacher, and that's the job I've been

doing my whole life. I've got a music degree from college and I went on to get a PGCE which is a postgraduate certificate of education. That was in classroom teaching, and I was intending to go into primary school teaching. When I left college, I applied for more than 60 jobs and went for a lot of interviews but never once got offered a job, and I think that's because I'm autistic. I know now that I'm just terrible at interviews. I had to think what else I can do, and I've been playing the piano since the age of five, so I thought I would try teaching it. I've been doing that now for 28 years. It's very energy draining, and some days I'm teaching all day. I work in a couple of schools, so it's four days out of five that I'm in schools, and then I work after school as well.

I think as a child I was actually a classic autistic person. Had I been at school now, I would get spotted at about age five I think, because I didn't play with other kids in the playground at primary school. I basically played on my own because I found their games were just too noisy, too boisterous. I was a very quiet child as well. I'd say I had selective mutism, and I often wouldn't talk. If someone asked me a question or asked me my name, I would answer, but other than that, there were times where I wouldn't talk all day.

I used to stim a lot. I would put my fingers on top of my shoulders and wiggle them around. I know it looks really weird, but I did that as a kid and I got the mickey taken out of me for it. I didn't even notice I was doing it until other kids pointed it out to me. So that had been an obvious sign. Also, I think because I was clever and I always did well at school, my autism didn't get picked up at the time. There wasn't even dyslexia and things like that. Kids were either clever or they were thick, and they got extra help if they needed extra help.

I loved school. I loved the work and the structure. I was weird in that I liked the things that other kids didn't like. I loved the maths, and the English, and assemblies when we went in to listen to the headmaster tell us a story – I really liked that. The other kids hated all the lining up and going in silence into the hall. I loved that, but when it got to playtime, I just wished that I could stay in and read a book, but we weren't allowed to do that.

The PE lessons, I absolutely hated as well because I was so bad at it. I was always the last to get picked for teams. They were always so noisy. The other kids, they liked the playtime and the PE lessons and hated everything else, but I was the opposite. I did really like everything else at school. And I liked the company of the teachers. I had some lovely teachers. I preferred talking to them than talking to the other kids.

It was hard during the teenage years because I was

pretty lonely. I went to a school which had a special music department, so I was very lucky in that. I auditioned for it at the age of 11 and got accepted, which meant that I got taken out of my class for about five hours a week for music tuition. I did piano, clarinet, choir, wind band and musicianship; we got all those extra lessons. And that was what really helped me because that was my thing that I was good at. I spent a lot of time practising, so I stayed in the music block by myself most break times practising, but it was noticeable that I didn't have friends for most of that time.

I would have liked to have help with social skills at that time, although I wouldn't have liked something that would mean I got bullied even more, because I was already called weird freak, and if there was something else that they could bully me about, probably they would have done. It was just verbal bullying. I'm lucky it didn't go to worse physical bullying, but it still hurts. I just got on with my work and tried to ignore them. That was the best way of dealing with it. The teachers, they didn't have anti-bullying week like they do now. I think teachers do a lot more now to stop that kind of thing, but in the 1980s they didn't.

As an adult, there were just little things where my wife Alex and I were clashing in our communication styles. My main autistic trait that I think I have now is alexithymia, which is where I really don't know what I'm feeling about things a lot of the time. I feel something but about three days later than the actual event, so that is possibly my most noticeable autistic trait now. That can be challenging in relationships if I don't know what I'm feeling about things.

My wife Alex said to me before the diagnosis, "I think you might be autistic. I've been reading about it. Would you think about getting an assessment?" So, I went to my GP initially, and she said, "Why would you want to get diagnosed? You've got a good job, a good relationship, and you've managed up to this time." And she said, "You'll be taking resources away from autistic children", which is ridiculous because it's a completely different service. Basically, the GP didn't have a clue, but I said, "I have a right to know if I'm autistic", so eventually I persuaded her to give me a referral to the adult autism service. Then I had to wait a full year. It's actually longer than a year now with the waiting list, but at that time it was a whole year, and I only just got in on a cancellation. Somebody rang me up that morning and said, "We've had somebody drop out, can you come along at ten o'clock this morning?" I did that and then I had to go to work later that day, so I only had half my interview that day, but they arranged another appointment with me six weeks later and then I got my diagnosis. It was a long process to get mine, but then Alex herself realised that she could be autistic too and so we were both diagnosed.

Receiving the diagnosis helped me understand myself a lot more. I read a lot of books about it now. Since my diagnosis, I've joined various groups and made a lot of friends who are also autistic, which is lovely. I've got more friends now than I've had at any other point in my life through the autism community.

I'm in a theatre group which actually rehearses just down the road from me. It's something I found after my diagnosis, and I've always been interested in theatre. This group, it's for autistic people and others. We are not all autistic in the group, but over half of us are, and the director, he is not autistic, but he worked in special education before he retired. Now he's retired, he puts all of his energy into this group, and he writes plays and scenes for us to do. It's been a really good thing to be involved in.

Also, there is a conference in the UK called Autscape. It happens once a year, although obviously it only happened online during Covid. There are about 200 to 300 autistic people who all get together for three days, and we have workshops and lectures and discussions. I've been three times in person now and twice online. I've met a lot of friends through the Autscape community.

Although I've made a lot of new friends, I'm not really a very social person. I don't mix with that many people face to face, other than Alex. However, my friends all know that I am autistic, even the neurotypical ones, and they're fine with that. And some people say, "You are just the same person, and it doesn't really matter, does it?"

And at the schools I work at, I haven't told them about my autism diagnosis because I don't feel that I need any special accommodations at the moment. I work in the schools on a self-employed basis, and I just go in and teach one or two children at a time, just me and them in one room. I don't have a great deal of interaction with the other staff.

Knowing that I am autistic has helped in my teaching. I've advertised myself as a teacher for neurodivergent students, and I'm teaching more autistic students now. One of them, he came to me aged nine and he stayed with me until he was 20 and he went on to music college. When he came aged nine, he could hardly speak, but he had perfect pitch and could play loads of things by ear. And three other teachers had already said that his style did not suit them, so they did not want to teach him. Then he came to me and felt comfortable with me. He didn't want to learn to read music. He had an amazing memory. He could just copy anything

I played and remember it forever, so he got to quite an advanced level. He took his grade eight exam with me without being able to read a note of music, just remembering everything.

I think because I'm autistic and he is too, that is how we really got along. I was absolutely the right teacher for him, and then one of his friends came to me, and in fact his friend has just come back to me now for a few lessons. He is in his final year at university and is just coming for a few brush-up lessons before his final recital, and so I'm still in touch with him. So that's really good.

As an autistic person, I have strengths in music, obviously. It's helped a lot. A lot of autistic people have very good hearing because of our sensory differences and hyper-focus, so music was always something I was really interested in. I hyper-focused on that when I was younger, which meant that I could get really good at it.

I'm good at time management as well, which helps in my business. I know a lot of autistic people do struggle with executive dysfunction and things, but that's not something I really struggle with. I was always very interested in time, and I enjoyed school because it was all in the timetable and I liked going to one room at 9 o'clock and another room at 10 o'clock and just knowing that that's going to happen. So I've always been good at that sort of thing.

The challenges for me: I did mention about alexithymia where I don't know what I'm feeling, which can be hard, and I do struggle with some sensory things. Especially as I've got older, I find things can be really quite painful if somebody is doing roadworks outside, or there are sirens going past. If I go into a busy café or bar, and there's loads of background noise and crockery and coffee machines, I find that really difficult. I can't stay more than about an hour in that sort of environment. I just say, "I'm sorry, I have got to go now."

I wish others knew that autism can be so different for different people. I met a lot of different autistic people who I actually feel I have nothing in common with. There are a lot of autistic people who are into sci-fi and *Doctor Who* and all that sort of thing. That doesn't interest me in the slightest.

It's just as I was saying about the differences between us. I've heard a lot of autistic people describe themselves, or people describe them, as difficult and dramatic. Those descriptions don't fit me. And lazy as well – that's another one I heard. I was actually the opposite of those things as a child. I was compliant and I was hard-working, and I was easy-going and yet was still autistic. There are that many differences.

CHAPTER 3

It wasn't me just being rubbish

Matilda

England · Diagnosed autistic at age 38

Matilda works as a lived experience professional in nursing education and lives with her husband, child and three cats. It was four cats, but one moved in with another family. He still comes to visit sometimes.

SO, I AM MATILDA. I currently work as a lived experience lecturer for a nursing programme in the UK. I have a daughter who is going to be ten next week. I have three cats, a husband and I have a long history of mental health issues. So, lots of anxiety, depression and then psychosis as well. I ended up having an episode of psychosis which was quite unpleasant and wound up on meds and stuff. It was interesting, because when I had the psychosis, I had a psychiatrist actually ask me,

"Has anyone ever suggested that you might be autistic?" I was just like, "No, I can't deal with this conversation right now. I am completely bonkers, I can't deal with this." So I kind of ignored it for a couple of years until I'd had a lot of therapy and I had gone through a lot of recovery with my mental health, and I got to the point where I was, like, I feel quite good but I've still got this stuff which is still here: I'm still having light sensitivity, I'm still having sound sensitivity, I'm still struggling with my social relationships and communication, but I don't feel like I'm unwell any more.

I was involved a lot in the mad community,* which does overlap with the autistic community, so I had people coming into my social media timeline talking about their experience as an autistic person and I'm going, "Oh, that's me. Is that weird? I thought that was normal. Doesn't everyone do that?" And that made me kind of think, actually I do need to have a look at this. I ended up getting diagnosed privately but it was really about me exploring my mental health, wanting to understand whether I was mad or I was autistic. Or both.

I see a lot of overlaps between the mad side and the autistic community and the activism. It's really interes-

---

* Reference to "mad" and "mad community" throughout this chapter and subsequent chapters is made in a non-ableist way where the participants use the word "mad" for themselves and embrace the label.

ting. There is quite a lot of overlap, also quite a lot of friction sometimes where there is stigma in both directions, but more and more people are starting to realise the link between mental health diagnosis and autism. A lot of autistic people often end up with a diagnosis like personality disorder, for example. I guess there is a real lack of understanding of autism within mental health services. To be honest, I don't think they're great at recognising it. And when they do recognise it, they're not great at supporting it and understanding that complexity that you can be autistic and have mental health issues, and those things can intertwine within a person and vice versa.

But there are a lot of people who don't get an autism diagnosis. I've worked in primary care in mental health support, and I had quite a number of people I worked with, who got to a point after talking for a while being asked, "Have you looked at autism?" And it was quite life-changing for them where, "Oh, oh, that makes sense." Because I think when you're told you have mental health issues and all the stuff that you find is difficult because of your mental health, you feel like you ought to get better. You feel like you're just not trying hard enough. But when it is not getting better when you're having your therapy and your treatment, it kind of becomes your fault when you're always working and trying to make it all go better and be normal, and when you get that diagnosis, you go, "That's okay, you're autistic." It's a real kind of relief, to be like, "Oh, I can stop trying so hard." Which I am never going to be able to do.

It's important that people are aware of what autism looks like, and I think a lot of the mainstream understanding of autism is complete tosh. Such as, "I do feel empathy so I can't be autistic." I think that a lot of autistic people almost have excessive amounts of empathy and actually become quite overwhelmed with the experience of other people's emotions. I think it's because we don't necessarily express that empathy and feeling in a way in which other people recognise or feel is right that they say we don't have it.

I find it really interesting the conversation around black-and-white thinking as well, and nuance and the idea that autistic people don't understand nuance, and then I think about how much we need specificity in questions and stuff. The reason why I need you to be really clear about questions is because I see all the nuance and that's why I need the clarity. It's not that I don't understand nuance – I totally see nuance. I see too much nuance that you don't recognise, and that's why I need you to be really clear with me when you ask me a question about something or when you want me to do something, because I'm going to go, "Yeah, what about this or this or this or this?"

We have a very strong feeling of justice and what is right or wrong, and people think you're very black-and-white and you don't understand nuance and stuff. No, I do understand nuance, but I also know I'm right. And I think the problem of this is that it challenges a lot of the patriarchal power relationships within the history of autism. For us as autistics to say, "Actually, no, you're wrong – all that stuff you've been saying is not how it is" – it challenges that whole foundation, like people's careers and sense of self and importance and identity, and that they are there to benevolently make our lives better by teaching us how to be more normal. They don't like that, so they just ignore us.

Looking back, my autistic traits and oddities got normalised by my parents who are like, "Everyone is a bit weird, that's fine." And also, there was a lot of other stuff going on. As a child, I was very self-contained within myself because of my sibling who was causing so much trauma and crisis. So I was very introverted and very quiet and very much like, "I must not cause a fuss." As a lot of autistic people do, I think.

There were definitely signs of autism growing up. Like when I was a child, I used to love stroking fish. It sounds really weird. My parents had to stop taking me to the fishmongers because I would pat the fish. It became a running joke. It was a sensory thing. I loved the feel of it. One of my brothers went through a fishing phase, and I used to like putting my hands in the maggots. I liked the touch of it and the sensory experience of these weird things.

As autism seems to run in families, often it's not recognised because parents are like, "That's normal. I feel like that too." So as a child, I kind of knew that I was weird, and I knew that I was a bit odd, but when I talked to my parents about that, it was always very much dismissed, which left me feeling like I don't quite fit but I should be able to. So as much as it's nice for people to go, "Oh no, you're normal, it's fine, it's completely normal to feel this way," at the same time, when you know that you don't fit, it leaves you feeling like it's your fault for not being able to cope and for not being able to feel okay about that. And I should feel okay. Everyone is telling me I'm normal; I should be able to feel okay, but I can't cope with this stuff that everyone else can cope with, so it must be my fault. And I think that it is an unintended consequence of people trying to be really nice to you and not diagnose and not make you feel weird. But you know you're weird.

I was always the slightly weird one at school, and all my friends, I can look back and tell, totally, they're neurodiverse. I had a chat with a friend who has recently been diagnosed with ADHD, and we were talking about when you form that identity as a person who is an outsider but not too outside. So you're like, I'm not part of any group but I try to maintain that line of not being too weird so you don't get completely bullied and picked on. And there's this space within social groups at school where "That's just Matilda. She's just a bit weird but not too weird." And I think that a lot of neurodivergent people float in that space of kind of cool weird, not too weird. So I never really had a social group, and the social groups that I did slide into were very much the outsider groups. If that makes sense.

My autism diagnosis changed things for me. I'd kind of thought it out and I went private for an assessment and paid ridiculous sums of money because it was a two-year to two-and-a-half-year wait here in the health system. It's bonkers. I was like, "I'm just going to go." But when I got the diagnosis, despite me kind of being pretty sure I was going to get it, it took me a long time to process that, and I think at first I kind of went, "I don't know what to do with this." As I processed it, it's helped me to understand what I need. And to be okay with that, to say, actually, this is the stuff that I can deal with, and this is the stuff that I can't deal with, and if I do start stuff which is going to burn me out, I am going to end up completely bonkers and so I can't do that. I learned to manage my boundaries and my limits, and it's given me that kind of understanding to do that, and I think that's been really useful. And slowly unmasking has been really interesting.

Unmasking for me is not feeling like I have to always make eye contact with people all the time. Actually, it's easier for me to just not do that. I'm not going to worry about it. Recognising that I can't manage these types of demands that you are putting on me. I'm not going to burn myself out trying to work in a situation which isn't going to fit me. Also, I don't go to social stuff as much any more. I don't enjoy it. I'm much happier knowing that I'm not going to the weird work pub meal thing, because otherwise I'm just going to sit there not hearing people and feeling awkward.

I can't filter out background noise, and when there are multiple people talking in restaurants, I'm just like, "That's too much effort." I think when you get to a number where there are multiple conversations happening, I never understand how to navigate that. How do you know what conversation you are supposed to be part of? Or not part of? Is it okay to just start talking to this person or not? Then people look at you like you're weird. How does this weird network thing work? I don't understand it. So I just don't try any more.

I think masking is a thing that I suspect all autistic people do to one degree or another on one level of success. I certainly did a lot of masking, and I think it was only after my diagnosis that I realised how much of it I did. For me, masking also means that I was very much pushing myself into social situations, trying to be a normal person, accepting discomfort in sensory situations, particularly noise and light sensitivity and uncomfortable clothes. Things like that. It's thinking that those were normal, and I just had to deal with them.

Whereas now I just don't do that. I think this is the case for a lot of autistic people. You become an expert on watching people and copying, so it tends to be a lot of mirroring, a lot of changing how you behave depending on who you are with. So I think I mask differently in different situations. And sometimes that's useful, being able to walk into a different situation and be someone who fits in there, but it's exhausting if you are doing it all the time and you don't recognise what you are doing.

I think it's a difficult thing to describe because when you are doing it, before I knew I was autistic, it was more like the fish in the water joke: the fish doesn't know how the water is because they are always in the water. That's just what it is. And that's how it is when you are doing it.

Even little things, like I find it really difficult to write notes and listen at the same time. So when I was at university, I would never write notes in lectures. And in meetings. At work, I go into meetings and I never take any notes. I stopped taking a notebook with me. And people would look at me really oddly, like I wasn't taking it seriously, that I wasn't properly engaging. So, after a while, I started taking my notebook and I would just leave it on the table. I wouldn't write anything in it, but if I had it with me, it was okay. It's a negotiation. I knew I would be more useful to them at that meeting if I wasn't writing notes because I knew that I would not be able to engage fully in that conversation if I was trying to write stuff down. But their expectation was that I should, that I wasn't serious if I wasn't. So you find this middle ground where I am not going to write notes but I will have the paraphernalia of note writing, so that you feel like I am taking it seriously.

I think it's a really good metaphor for masking because you do it to make other people comfortable, and you get to the point where you are balancing what you can do, what you can manage, so that you can live your life with what other people need you to be in order for them to be comfortable. And that might not be at all helpful for you, or even allow you to achieve the things that they want you to achieve, so you are always walking the balance between being able to do stuff the way you need to do it and presenting the paraphernalia that makes other people feel more comfortable.

Now that I know about masking, it was a big thing to realise that it wasn't me just being rubbish; it wasn't just that I couldn't cope. And now I can make a choice to a degree as to whether I mask or not mask and how much I mask. I'm much more aware of when I am masking, whereas before it was an automatic thing that you just do. I think I am becoming more able to make choices around when I mask and how much I mask.

It's always interesting watching people's reactions to me not masking. And then my reactions to their reactions and how you kind of manage that. It does add a whole other level of emotional work to my job. I was talking to my manager about the added burden that you have when you are a lived experience professional because you're taking yourself into a job. It's much more personal and much more difficult.

I think masking and burnout are linked. I think often the pressure that we feel to do things in an acceptable way to meet other people's standards and to work in a way that doesn't work for us because we are trying to mask, because we are trying to fit in, is often what results in a burnout. Before I got my diagnosis, I became more and more aware that having a disconnect between how I am feeling inside and having to present in a different way makes me really unwell. Having to do things that I don't feel comfortable with, that don't align with my values, often leads to burnout because I find that really difficult and really exhausting. I think masking is a situation where you are being incongruent – you are acting all the time, even if you don't realise you are doing it – and that is emotionally difficult and exhausting, and I think there is often a level of moral injury to that as well. I mean, you are pressured to act in ways that you don't feel comfortable with and that you don't feel are appropriate. I had big issues in my last job when I was managing a team, and my manager wanted me to manage my team and do things in ways that I felt were morally not right. I was like, "No I can't do that. That is not appropriate and I'm not going to do that." Then I think it was that autistic sense of justice, of having really strong values, and then you are trying to balance that to try to fit in and be normal and mask; it can result in a moral injury.

I think the biggest benefit of diagnosis is it gives you permission to go, "This is just how it is." And it doesn't matter how much work I put in, that's not going to change, so I have permission to change my life to work for me rather than trying to change me to work for my life. I think, honestly, the autism diagnosis has been really positive. It's really helped with my husband, for me to be a bit clearer with him about what works for me and what doesn't. And for him to be clearer with me for what works for him and what doesn't. And for us to have that conversation around what we need. I think it has been really positive.

I'm more aware of the risk of burnout too. I will never work full-time again because it always leaves me burning out every time. And I am very conscious of what I need to maintain my wellness, and the space I need and the time I need for myself, and what I can and can't do, and what my priorities are. Because the consequences of burnout are so severe for me, I'm really strict with myself now. I'm not doing that again. I have to be constantly balancing a little bit and questioning, "Is that realistic? Am I going to have space to look after myself? Am I going to be able to do that and be well?" So, it's kind of an ongoing process, I think.

I think, like a lot like autistic people, when I get excited about stuff, I take on lots of stuff. I'll be like, "Yeah, that's so cool, I want to do all the cool stuff right now." I take on loads and loads and loads of stuff which is all really cool, and I want to do it all, but it gets too much and then I become completely overwhelmed. I get a lot of depression and anxiety around it, and I will find it increasingly difficult to even communicate. My daughter describes it as like not being able to get her words out, and it's like that when your brain is working but there are no words coming out in the way you want them to.

And I get psychosis, so for me one of the things that happens is I will start getting visual symptoms like blurred vision. I will get your classic wobbly walls and breathing, and I get a lot of derealisation, so a lot of the feeling that things aren't real, and depersonalisation like I'm just riding around in my body. And then if I keep pushing myself, I start properly hallucinating. I have had periods where it's been like everything is made out of paper. And my last one was where there were loads of fake trees and plants everywhere – it was quite beautiful. I get quite euphoric when I hallucinate. I'm like, "Yeah, it's so beautiful, it's really pretty. I'm fine, don't worry about it, it's fine." Because I get really euphoric, I don't reach out for help at that point because I'm very much like, "I am fine, I'm just in my world. It's cool." One time, I ended up with a lot of paranoia and a lot of delusional thinking and lots of really horrible, unpleasant things. And then I broke down and I had to take a year out. I spent a year being bonkers, doing a lot of therapy. Medication for the first half. For me, burnout is like a progressive thing, and I have to be really aware of those initial warning signs because I know what it ends like. And for me, the end was not nice.

I am very aware of my initial warning signs and my triggers now, so I have to be really careful when I get into that autistic "Yeah, this is so cool, I want to do everything." I have to be like, "No, Matilda." And my husband's quite good; he's like, "Are you sure? Can you do that?" So I'm really aware of my triggers and warning signs, and I have to be constantly watching myself and aware of when I let myself go a little bit wild and when I have to be, "No, that's too much." It's taken a lot of therapy, and a lot of time to kind of get those skills, and it's a constant working thing, but I think when you have a long-term thing, when you can't cure it, all you can do is learn how to manage it. And so that's what I've had to do.

I think as I speak to more and more autistic people who were diagnosed later, they grew up feeling very alone. They thought they were the only people who felt that way, the only people to have that experience. The only people who couldn't fit and couldn't cope. I remember really well having a period where I was thinking, "Everyone else can cope with life and I can't. Why can't I deal with stuff that everyone else can deal with?" And the shame of that and the feeling that it was my fault, whereas actually, if I had known that I was autistic, I'd know that there are lots of people who can't cope with that, and that's fine. I'm not on my own with stuff that I find difficult. There are thousands of people who also find this stuff difficult, and I'm not just some rubbish person who just can't deal with the normal things of life, and I ought to be able to do that. And I think that's really important for people. For the vast majority of autistic people I have spoken to, having their diagnosis has been overwhelmingly positive and has made sense of stuff. And I think, why would we deny people that?

Because I've been diagnosed quite recently, and because of my mental health stuff, I'm still kind of working through what things are autistic and how those present and whether they are strengths or not. And a lot of whether it is a strength or not is how you use something. Like attention to detail can be really useful in particular situations, and other times it can be overwhelming and a mess. My autism gives me a different way of looking at the world. And even before I was diagnosed, I was always aware that I came at things from a different angle to other people. I think that can have its difficulties, but also it means that I am good at problem-solving.

Some of the struggles I have with autism are around communication, and I have very strong ideas about what is right. I've had some issues at work recently around meeting times. They have this 8.30am meeting and I'm like, "Eight thirty in the morning is not an okay time to have a meeting. That's not accessible." I take medication which makes me tired in the morning, and we've got people in the team that have various health issues. Like, yeah, we can drag ourselves out, but we shouldn't have to. It's just the principle of it not being accessible and not okay. That has caused issues with people.

I also find that people, neurotypical people, just totally make amazing leaps of understanding in completely weird directions. You say one thing, and suddenly it turns into this whole personal attack. And you're like, "That isn't what I said at all." At one meeting, I had to go, "Can we stop for a minute because I don't know how we have got to this conversation?" I don't understand what I am defending myself against, so I think sometimes that communication difference is that people can take what I perceive as just a thing that I'm saying, and they attach all this different meaning to it, which I'm sure makes sense to them within their understanding, but it was not attached to what I said. I find that difficult.

And I can get quite overwhelmed by sounds, noise and sensory sensitivities. These have been quite tiresome sometimes and the anxiety that comes along with that. They feed off each other so that when I'm anxious, my sensory sensitivities get worse. My light sensitivity gets much worse when I'm not in a good place, and then, of course, that sensitivity to light and touch, it just makes you more anxious and stressed, so it becomes like this vicious circle. To reset, I find dealing with the anxiety is the best approach. I will usually do whatever I need to do with the sensitivities, and then try to work out what is going on that is making me feel so stressed out.

One of the biggest impacts of having my autism diagnosis has been me giving myself permission to just be okay with my sensory needs and wear my sunglasses all the time even if it's cloudy, whereas before I thought I shouldn't. I felt like it wasn't okay for me to do stuff. So I've decided I'm actually going to wear my sunglasses, and I'm going to wear clothes that I find comfortable and stop feeling like I've got to conform to some weird uniform that's really horrible. I don't want to do that. I want elasticated waists and pockets. And I got myself a weighted blanket and it's like, "Oh my god, this is amazing."

And fidget toys. Before I got my diagnosis, I thought these things weren't for me; they were for other people. And since I've got the diagnosis, I'm like, actually, maybe they are for me, and they really help. I can read books and do stuff and focus when I've got a fidget toy, and I can feel so much more comfortable in bed with my weighted blanket. I think I've become much more able to look after myself and my sensory stuff since I've had my diagnosis.

With my diagnosis, it took me a long time to disclose it to my family. And actually, I don't think I've told my sister yet. I told my brother really recently, like a couple of weeks ago. It took me three months to tell my dad, and I see him most. It took me a while to feel comfortable because I needed to process it. When it comes to work, when I first got the autism diagnosis, I wasn't in this job, and I did disclose it to people at work because I think it helped them to work with me a bit. And with this job, it is part of my job to disclose my stuff. I think it's easier to disclose to people at work than with my own family. There are whole historical complexities with family. In fact, when I've told people I'm autistic, people have gone, "Oh yeah. That makes sense." I'm like, "What!? Why didn't anyone mention this? You're not even a little bit shocked." Everyone has been really supportive and cool about it. But a part of me is like nobody, not a single person, has said, "Oh, I don't think so, you don't seem autistic," which I think says something, doesn't it?

I'd love people to know about how autism affects day-to-day life. For example, I don't do big supermarkets. I can do little ones. I went through a stage where I was having a lot of panic attacks in supermarkets. I went and got cognitive behavioural therapy and it really helped. I was getting really bad social anxiety at the time, and

I would go into the shop, and I would put stuff in my basket and have a meltdown, and leave everything and go home. I would tell my poor husband we haven't got anything for dinner because I couldn't do the shops. He was like, "We'll get fish and chips."

I want people to listen to autistic people because the myths that have been created around what it is to be autistic are just so damaging and so much rubbish. Autism is a really good example of that kind of difference between experiential knowledge and learned knowledge. So you have all these people who sat down and studied autistic people like we're animals without ever actually talking to the autistic people, asking them or communicating with them. So all their knowledge on autism was based on observation and based on their interpretation of that behaviour. It was all learned knowledge, not experiential knowledge. And then you've got the autistic people going, "My experience is not that at all." I think it is an amazing example of the limitations of learned knowledge when you listen to the experience of the actual people living that. It's a vastly different world from what the people who sat and studied it thought.

CHAPTER 4

A diagnosis is an intervention in itself

Rebecca

Australia · Diagnosed autistic at age 32

Rebecca's special interests include yoga, psychology, spirituality and religion. Rebecca is still waiting for the hobby horse that she has been asking for each Christmas since she was a child.

> **Content warning:** Mentions suicide

MY EARLIEST MEMORY is when I was three years old, watching *Thomas the Tank Engine*. I always loved trains, and I loved *Thomas the Tank Engine*, and I would play with my brother's train set all the time and make different train tracks all throughout our house. But I don't really remember having a lot of imaginative play. People would give me Barbie dolls and stuff like that, and I'd be like, "What's this? What do you do with this?" I thought, this is really boring, and I was really struggling to make up social scripts for the Barbie dolls interacting with each other, whereas I was really drawn to active play like climbing trees, jumping on the trampoline, digging in the sandpit, and I would really be drawn to playing with the boys. I found in primary school when I was younger, having friendships with boys was a lot easier for me than with girls because we shared more interests, and I was more of a tomboy in primary school.

In primary school, I read obsessively. My mum reckons that when I was a baby, she would literally find me in my cot with my dummy* reading the little wooden books that I would be given as a kid. She had to take me to the library three or four times a week and just constantly supply me with new books. By grade three, I was reading *Lord of the Rings*, the three books in three days. And I had a really advanced vocabulary but not so much of an understanding of the advanced words that I was using. I definitely had hyperlexia.

Also, I took things very literally. I remember having fights with the kids in the class about how they didn't pronounce words correctly, and kids would play pranks and I'd fall for them and then get in trouble with the teacher for falling for them. So, this kid in our class

---

* Pacifier.

pretended to faint. I was like, "Oh my god, Mrs so-and-so, this kid's fainted," and then he just got up. And I'm the one that got in trouble for getting upset about it. I really thought he fainted – "Why am I getting punished for this?"

And it's interesting, my mum and I went through my school report cards in the lead up to me getting my diagnosis. I always got really good grades at school, and I kind of felt like there wouldn't be any comments in my report cards, but when we actually looked at the report cards, there were heaps of comments pointing to my development being a little bit different. And both my mum and I were shocked that she hadn't really picked up on it. She just didn't know, and because I was getting good grades, I think it wasn't really being paid attention to, but they were heaps of comments about not listening to instructions properly, not paying attention in class. So whenever I got bored because the class was moving at too slow a pace, I would just read novels under my desk. Then I wasn't allowed to read novels, so the only books that I was allowed to read in class were the Dictionary, Thesaurus and the Bible. So I read them all cover to cover several times in class because, again, I was bored.

I also had comments in my report card about being too talkative. They called me unique. They said I had excellent recall of facts, excellent vocabulary, and "sometimes becomes totally absorbed in a particular activity and she needs rousing". Apparently, I was still talking in baby talk in grade two and there were a lot of comments about me not asking for help, becoming silly and noisy in class, needing to stay calm and speak quietly, needing to become more aware of the needs of others. I was called attention seeking, I needed to mature, I didn't accept correction, and I was more confident when telling my personal experiences than creating imaginary stories.

I think on some deep level I knew that I was different and didn't fit in during primary school, but I don't think I was super aware of it because I didn't actually get bullied about being different. Some of the kids in the class would say, "Rebecca the freak, Rebecca the geek." And I'd be like, "Rebecca the unique." It never really hurt my feelings. I kind of just brushed it off and that was really the extent of any bullying. My dad was the local doctor in a small country town, and I think that a lot of the parents looked up to him and respected him. I think I was sort of protected from bullying in the small Catholic primary school because the kids were told to be nice to me. The two friends that I had were young boys who were the other social outcasts. We would spend time in the library together and read and draw and stuff like that rather than play with the other kids.

In high school, I definitely got a rude shock because I went through three different friendship groups in three years in high school. I went from that small Catholic primary school to a really large state school, and it was quite rough. I got bullied in grade eight, my lunch got stolen, my lunch money was taken. I was threatened with being beaten up. The first group of kids that I tried to make friends with were quite rough and I would get made fun of a lot for not knowing colloquialisms that they all knew. They would talk about 50 Cent's newest song, and I would be like, "Who is 50 Cents?" I had no clue. I literally existed in my own little time zone of listening to Vivaldi and reading *Jane Eyre*. I didn't know what was going on socially that most of the other teenagers were interested in talking about. Toward the end of grade ten, I ended up spending a lot of time in the library and really being confused. "How do other people know what to do and say? How come I keep offending people when I open my mouth and say stuff? Why do I keep losing friends?"

Then my parents divorced, and we ended up moving: just me, my mum and my brother for grade 11 and 12. I went to a different school that was a private high school, more affluent, and I didn't get bullied there. All the kids were really quite all right, quite nice, but I was seen as a weirdo, so I always floated in the nerd girl group because I found it easier to fit in there and be really nerdy myself. I just remember walking through school and people would be like, "Her face is really flat. She is not smiling, she is not having facial expressions." Or people would think I was a bitch or an ice queen because I was very sarcastic and had no facial expression.

When I started that new school, I was determined that this time I was going to make friends, this time I was going to learn how to be a cool girl and not lose these friendships. By that time, in grade 11 and 12, I was more socially aware, and I would copy what the other girls would say and do. I'd copy their outfits and hair and their make-up but still never quite get it right. Because I was getting good grades and I was okay-looking, I guess I had a bit of privilege to kind of pass. I was deemed the funny kid as well and made jokes about things; I was like the weird, hippie, funny girl. That's how I was portrayed.

I would go to the library and literally get out *How to Win Friends and Influence People,** or read books on body language, and then a friend in high school was going to study psychology, and I was like, oh my god, I'll study psychology. That's how I'll learn how to be perfect. That's how I'll learn how other people think

---

* *How to Win Friends and Influence People* is by Dale Carnegie.

and then I won't ever make these social mistakes again. Then, in year 12, my boyfriend, who was also not neurotypical, ended up developing schizophrenia while we were dating, and he had to drop out of school because even though he was very smart and a lovely guy, he just wasn't able to maintain the schooling. I went down a rabbit hole of researching schizophrenia and getting really interested in psychology and how to help him, and that's what started that special interest of people and psychology.

I would say the first actual real friendship that I made was in my first job out of university, with a girl I've been friends with now for 12 years. She has an autistic brother who is on the disability pension. She acknowledged that she is probably autistic as well, but she and I got on. She was my only friend for years. Then, during my master's, I had another friend who is 20 years older than me. She's now getting tested for ADHD. The other friendships that I ended up making were through some of those friends. I think I feel comfortable because everyone around me is neurodivergent, so I don't have to be somebody else. And I think my masking was never that great anyway, to be honest. My bosses and my colleague picked it up even though I was trying super hard; I think people had a sense that I am different or I am unique, and some people have found that a really positive attribute and some people have seen it as threatening, or they are not comfortable with it because I think about things differently than they do. I've always been told, "You think too much. You think about things too deeply. Why can't you just relax and take it easy?" I'm like, that's not me, I'm always analysing. I'm always observing. I'm always noticing the patterns in things and how things relate. People don't like that sometimes, but that's their problem. I constantly need to feed my brain.

I do just want to add one more thing about childhood stuff. I do think living in a country town also contributed to me not having as many difficulties as I would have if I had grown up in a city. We lived on an acreage which meant that we had no neighbours. It was quiet, peaceful; we never had people over to our house. My dad wasn't very social. I never had sleepovers and people come over. And I feel like the primary school I went to as well, it was super small, had small classes, very quiet, lots of nature. If I had grown up in a big city with all the busyness, the traffic, noise, the bigger schools, noisier classrooms, I think that I would have had more sensory issues and meltdowns.

In my journey to diagnosis, my employment as a psychologist played a part. I work in a group private practice, and our boss is openly ADHD. She is a neuropsychologist, and a lot of the team are ADH-Ders, but I'm the only one who is openly autistic on the team. I mainly work with adults, and that's because even as a kid, I always felt more comfortable around adults than people my own age. I have always tended to get along better with people either a lot older than me or a lot younger than me. It's like, if I didn't really understand children when I was a child, what hope do I have now? And I had to spend so long learning my therapy skills, of how to communicate with other adults, and refining my therapy techniques for working with adults, that the thought of having to go through that whole process again, of learning how to interact with children, is too overwhelming. I'm just going to stick with adults.

My bread and butter, or what I've been interested in, is doing trauma therapy, and having some side interests in chronic pain, sleep and chronic illness. Those kind of go together with trauma. My boss – her special interest is in autism and ADHD, and particularly in girls. When I first got registered as a psychologist, I went along to the work training about autism in adults and what it is like in women. We never really learned about that at university in psychology, even though I did six years at university and a master's in clinical psychology. It was all about children and from a very limited perspective.

So I rock up to this training and they go through what women on the spectrum look like, from when they are little kids through to adulthood. And everything they said was really resonating, and it was like a lightbulb moment for me: "Oh my god, am I on the spectrum?" And at the time, I knew that my partner, who is now my husband, was on the spectrum. I had gone and read books and stuff on how to help him, but I had never thought to apply it to myself because it was all very male-centric and very typical information focused on men on the spectrum.

In the training, it was said that if you have childhood trauma, then it can look like you are on the autism spectrum, but you might not actually be on the autism spectrum. This resonated with me because I have had a difficult childhood background as well – there was some domestic violence for me growing up. So, for me, I was like, "Okay, how can I be a psychologist and I'm registered, I've gone through all this training, and how can I do that and be autistic and no one have picked it up or diagnosed me? Can I actually be autistic?" I thought, maybe it's childhood trauma, then. And I went and did my own trauma therapy. A few years later after going through all this trauma therapy I was like, well, all these quirks and traits are still present. I have gone and done all this trauma therapy, and I really feel like I have resolved my childhood trauma the best I can, but I still have a lot of autistic traits.

Then, a couple of years ago, I noticed a lot more information in books and resources that were on the affirming side coming out and more books about autistic presentations in women. And my colleague recommended that I read a book called *Neurotribes*.* And that really shifted my beliefs and ideas on autism from the very limited stuff we learned at university to having a more affirming viewpoint and starting to accept that, okay, I really think I'm on the autism spectrum. And I probably have a sprinkling of ADHD as well.

That started me off on going into a deep dive. It became my special interest where I was reading up on it, obsessed with it. I ended up getting my official diagnosis a couple of years ago now, and that was just really helpful because even for myself as a psychologist, I was still having a lot of doubts like, "Am I just faking it? Am I doing this for attention? Am I making all this up?" And I really needed that outside confirmation. I sort of came out at work and mentioned it to my boss who is the ADHDer and my clinical supervisor who had supervised me through my registrar programme at that practice, who is also an ADHDer. And they both had said

---

* The full title of this book is *Neurotribes: The Legacy of Autism and How to Think Smarter About People Who Think Differently* by Steve Silberman.

that they noticed autistic traits in me because they have children that are ADHD and autistic. But they hadn't said anything to me. And my colleague, she does autism and ADHD assessments in women for a living, and she's like, "Oh, yeah, you are so autistic." For myself, I've learned a lot of skills in how to mask and stuff like that, especially through my degree, but she said it's really obvious. And I was like, "Is it?" Okay.

But I do wish I had known about my diagnosis earlier in some ways. I think it would have been really difficult for me to accept it as a teenager, if I had found out as a teenager. But if I had found out as a young child, I think it would have really helped me to understand myself better and not put so much pressure on myself, and accept myself. I think I would have struggled a lot less in terms of maybe not forcing myself to have to mask as much. Potentially, my health may have not been as badly affected by pushing myself and then getting burnt out. Maybe I wouldn't have had such bad health challenges as I have now that still affect me.

I really wish that I had got a lot more support as a child in primary school but I think too, because I was in primary school in the early 1990s, if I had been diagnosed then, the support that I would have had, I don't know that it would have been helpful because it would have been more based around forcing you to be a neurotypical person and masking. I kind of feel like it would have been better if I had been born now, maybe. And then had the benefit of the whole neurodiversity movement. I think it would have alerted my mum and dad to the fact that I needed support because I was sort of the kid who didn't cause too much trouble at home, and more attention was given to my brother who was probably more externalising, whereas I was probably more internalising. I think because I was a girl as well, I didn't get as much support, and then I think because of the giftedness as well, I didn't get as much support.

But maybe I had to come to it in my own time as well, with my own level of realisation or readiness to accept it. I think if I had been told that information without having all of those affirming resources behind me, and that more affirming viewpoint that it is actually okay to be autistic, or to be an ADHDer, I think I would have had a lot more shame or ableist beliefs about it. Getting my diagnosis from the background of affirming litera-ture and resources, it actually helped me to accept my-self a bit. I've always had certain things that I struggle with, even though, not to toot my own horn, I am in that gifted category as well. So I do have the twice ex-ceptionality which I think has helped me overcome cer-tain difficulties or compensate for certain things. But it has also meant that I haven't really been recognised for what I have struggled with, or I've never really got help. I'd always excelled academically but not socially. My emotional development – I had to go to therapy to learn that and work on that as an adult. As I got older, my special interest shifted to human beings and psychology. I felt like if I had a different special interest, if I wasn't interested in people, then it would have been a lot more obvious as well. It's been interesting.

I feel getting my diagnosis of autism – and I don't have an official diagnosis of ADHD but I think that's definitely there too – helped me to drop a lot of the perfectionism and be kinder to myself and actually really accept, okay, this is why I am different, or this is why I struggle in certain areas, or this is why I have difficulty working full-time. And I always have. It gave me permission to be myself a lot more. More than traditional therapy ever did, actually. To me, getting a diagnosis is an intervention in itself.

The diagnosis of autism helped me to accept myself more. It helped me accept the people in my family as well, who are neurodivergent. It helped me to accept my husband and my relationship more. Helped me to accept that if I have kids, I'll likely have neurodivergent kids, and that will actually be really cool. And if I had a neurotypical kid, I don't know what I'd do, probably. I think it's just helped me to give myself permission to set up a life for me that works for me and I don't have to fit into those neurotypical norms. I think it's been really helpful as well just to learn about the sensory overload and the autistic burnout side of things too. Because I definitely battled with that over the years without really knowing what it was. If I make a social mistake, I don't feel bad about it. Just a lot of self-acceptance, which has been really helpful.

I do think having the ability to intellectually know what is expected and learn that, and then being able to mask, probably helped me to get further in the workplace than I would have if I didn't or couldn't mask. I do think that, even though I tried really hard, there were still times where people could tell I was different or I responded differently. In one of my first jobs, I worked in a prison, and the two counsellors at the prison were quite rough and would swear all the time. I thought how they acted was quite unprofessional according to the code of conduct. Also, I was the only person who would actually read through all of the rules to know what was expected of me because I like that certainty and knowing you're not going to get in trouble. So when I brought up that the swearing really bothers me and I don't think it's very professional – "We are in a government workplace; I don't want to have to be listening to you swear all the time because it is an open office"

– they got really offended because they thought I called them unprofessional. And then these two counsellors proceeded to bully me for the rest of the time that I was working there. I think it's things like that where you are the person who speaks up and says things that other people let slide or they play office politics, and I'm really bad about playing office politics or understanding the hidden messages and gameplaying that is going on.

Even now, working with clients and being in a leadership position, I'm now supervising other psychologists and I have had to learn to moderate my feedback because my natural tendency is to be quite blunt and call a spade a spade, but other people don't tend to react well to that. Unless they prefer that blunt feedback themselves, and I've noticed that a lot of neurodivergent people can also be very sensitive to any perceived criticism, but they also do appreciate honest feedback as well. They prefer that to not being clear.

I think masking definitely has served me well, but I think it has come at a cost. It is exhausting, and I've been going through the process of my own diagnosis of looking at how much do I unmask versus do I show my authentic self, and then how much is that actually going to cost me in terms of my work and my income and friendships and things like that. To me personally, I think it's a little bit of a compromise, but also because I think I've been quite honest about my diagnosis of being autistic, I think that is helpful in terms of being myself.

I'm lucky because most of my friends and my boss and my colleagues, my husband, they are all neurodivergent themselves. So me being myself, I feel like I have always kind of been that weirdo who has always been different and I haven't had to unmask a lot around friends. It's just been more admitting when you cancel at the last moment, or change plans at the last minute, it actually takes me the whole day to recover from that. Usually, I would keep those reactions hidden because of not wanting to hurt other people's feelings, or not knowing why I would have such a big reaction to a change in plan or people cancelling things. I think some of my friends, who were mostly also psychologists, were a little bit shocked. It's funny because I have a friend who works in the area of diagnosis and assessment, and she was like, "I don't see you being autistic," and I was like, "That's because I haven't shown you. Because I mask."

I think masking has contributed to burnout, but I think it's probably not the only thing that's contributed to burnout. I think it is just pushing myself to function according to neurotypical standards. Like when I was younger, I think I worked full-time for a couple of years, and that in itself was just too stressful and draining.

I need a lot more rest to recover from things than other people do. And social interaction plays a role in that. So normally on my days off, I often have to ration out how much I'm socialising and interacting with people versus spending time alone silent and recuperating, doing things that align with my other interests. I think masking definitely played a role in burnout, and it's quite interesting because there is a history of burnout in my family. My grandfather basically got a bunch of health conditions and burnt out from his job when he was 50 and had to have an early medical retirement. My dad burnt out at 40 and retired from being a doctor because he couldn't cope with it, and couldn't cope with life, couldn't cope with juggling working full-time and having a family, and not pursuing his interests. So, he's been on a disability pension for the past 20 years and hasn't really worked. And then I burnt out at 23 during my master's.

I think I burnt out during my master's because, unlike my first degree, during my master's I had friendships that I was trying to maintain. I had a relationship, a romantic relationship with my now-husband. I was living out of home, being independent and working part-time and trying to do my master's, so I think I was just trying to tackle too many things at once, and then I got a bunch of health conditions and unfortunately my health has never been the same. I have autoimmune diseases and chronic health conditions which now mean that I can't do as much. And I never have been able to since my burnout.

I had to take a year off my master's and really pull back and just not do a lot, and then go to working four days a week when I graduated and be more careful about how I spend my energy, and saying no to more things, knowing that I need more rest. And I think for me, having the physical health conditions helped people to accept that I can't do as much as other people do. Because at the time, I didn't have my autism diagnosis, so people would ask me, "Why aren't you working full-time?", and I'm like, "I just can't." I never returned to the level of functioning that I had because I think that was never my true level of functioning. I think that I'd always been pushing through, and pushing and pushing, and I don't think that was sustainable for me.

To prevent burnout, or recover from burnout, usually I go to my bedroom; my bedroom is my safe space. I lie in bed with dim lighting and not a lot of noise. Then I usually just read or watch my favourite TV shows and rest all day. And when I've had a week where I've got more fatigue, I don't do as many chores or cooking or housework, and I minimise my social interaction.

I really enjoy my work. My work is my special interest,

so I'm often very animated at work. It's not masking to me; it's because it's my passion. But still, interacting with people is draining. So at home, I often don't do anything on weeknights. The thought of going out again and socialising on weeknights is horrible. I don't know how people do that. On weeknights, I usually chill and relax and don't talk to anyone. I have periods of being mute, which really helps. I find that very restful.

Other ways of taking care of myself include wearing ear plugs when I go out. I will also be careful about where I go out. If my friends want to meet up, I'll look at the location and try to make it a less busy, noisy area. Going to a massive shopping centre would be my idea of a nightmare, or I know I will only be able to stay for a couple of hours and then have to leave. I wouldn't be able to do a whole-day shopping trip or something like that.

I really enjoy spending time in nature. That's very grounding and calming. And I do a lot of yoga and meditation as well. That's a mini special interest that I have. Because I was so obsessed with that, I ended up doing a bunch of yoga teacher training as well in different areas of yoga. I think that definitely helps. But I am very careful about my environment. Even my environment at work, I think it works for me because it's not noisy, I have control over my room, I have control over how many clients I see. I literally will have a nap in my breaks if I need to. I have control over my home environment. I stick to my routines. I mostly go to the same places and do the same things that I am comfortable with, with the same people. So I think all of that really helps.

I think with burnout too, just finding those ways of having a routine and having executive functioning strategies is really important. I've got my calendar and my diary, and I try to make sure not to overload my schedule too much. But there was a time, I think earlier this year, because I was getting so burnt out, I actually was having a lot of difficulty with cooking and cleaning, and I ended up literally eating white, bland foods. That was the first time I understood why autistic kids just eat their fish fingers or the white bland foods, and it's because anything else is too sensory overwhelming to deal with when you are stressed. It was the first time I had connected those dots together. But I had always had food things, like different foods that I had never liked eating. As a kid, I never liked eating a lot of dairy. I never liked to eat meat because it had a slimy feeling to it, like the fat on the meat – I would always cut all the fat off. I didn't like certain vegetables. I love fruit. I ate a lot of carbs as a kid, pasta and stuff like that. I think I was eating a lot of cheese toasties. Because I am gluten-free and dairy-free, due to food intolerances and IBS, I was eating a lot of vegan mac and cheese. Just eating a lot of easy-to-prepare food. The thought of preparing stuff was really overwhelming, so I think that at those times, knowing that it's okay, just not beating yourself up about it is really important. I try to have compassion for myself during those times.

I do practise a lot of self-compassion exercises, which is why I think I don't have a lot of shame and guilt over a bunch of things, and why I think my self-worth has generally been okay throughout my life. I think a lot of autistic people go through life with a lot of shame and guilt and low self-worth because of all the negative feedback they receive. I really like an activity I learned from Kristin Neff. She's got a book about self-compassion,* and it's like talking to yourself as though a friend is talking to you, rather than how your inner critic would usually talk to you. Just saying reassuring things like, "It's going to be okay, you're going to get through this. I know it's really hard right now but you'll be okay." Having empathy for yourself. And I'll often put my hand on my heart, and I imagine kindness and compassion going from my hand into my heart and soothing

---

* The title of this book is *Self-Compassion: The Proven Powers of Being Kind to Yourself* by Kristin Neff.

it as well. I think that's really helped me unpack some of the perfectionism and let go of a lot of that.

I've had lifelong anxiety. It's always been there, and knowing that that's linked to autism as well was quite helpful as a way of understanding. I think difficulty coping with change is very challenging. I had a hard time coping with the Covid pandemic because of the constant changes in routine. One moment we were locked down and then the next moment this was happening. It was all very unpredictable. That definitely caused a few meltdowns.

I think too, just worrying about being able to cope with things like having children or growing older. What will old age look like for me if I can't work full-time? Will I be able to afford a retirement? Things like that. Will my health get worse as I age? I think about things like that a lot. And just coping with the change that comes along with that. Because again, I'm very much a forward thinker. I think far ahead. And the statistics for autism aren't great. I don't know if you have come across them, but basically at the moment the statistics say that if you are autistic, it takes up to 20 years off your lifespan. So the average age that people live is in their 60s. There are a few reasons for that research figure. I think off the top of my head, it's to do with having a higher rate of suicide, having a higher rate of mental health issues, and also not accessing physical health care and not having healthcare providers who believe people when they are unwell and are in pain because they are not showing pain and things like that. And also because there is a link between being autistic and having more chronic health conditions, and health conditions in general and neurological conditions. So I think for someone like me, I don't shy away from things that people are uncomfortable looking at. To me, it is a legitimate worry. Am I going to have a lesser lifespan than other people because of being autistic and living in this society?

I think most people who are autistic don't want to be cured or fixed. There is this obsession with throwing all of these resources at people before they turn 18 so that magically they are not going to be autistic any more once they turn 18. And there is no help and support for adults because by then it's like, "It's too late, they are autistic now." Or, "Oh no, we've magically turned them into a neurotypical person so they don't need any help any more." Just getting support from a young age but knowing that you are going to continue to need support as an adult is really important. And where is the support for adults? Where is the recognition for adults? We are still struggling. In a lot of ways, life gets better after school, but you also have more expectations and responsibilities as well, with less support.

There's this whole idea, too, that if you are level one autism, you don't need any support. That's actually not true. A lot of the people I work with are level one, and they are really struggling. They are burnt out, they are trying to act like neurotypical people, and it's just not working for them. I would like to see more support across all the levels. It's just sort of like, "We don't want to be changed, we don't want to be fixed, we want to be supported and accommodated."

I think, too, if you are going through the process of diagnosis, a lot of people will have self-doubts and gaslight themselves, and go, "Am I autistic? Am I not?" I think when you get your official diagnosis, just give yourself six months to a year to process that. People process a lot of things leading up to the diagnosis, but then after the diagnosis there is a lot to unpack and process. And people will go back and review all these things from their childhood, all through their lives, and go, "This is why I reacted in this way." I think it's just important to give yourself space and compassion during that time.

I think there are a lot of autistic and ADHD health professionals and mental health professionals out there who are afraid to more openly disclose their neurodiversity because of fear of professional backlash. And there always is a risk. I am taking a risk by being open in the psychology community about being autistic, but I guess it is just a risk I am willing to take.

CHAPTER 5

Into the woods

Sydney

England · Diagnosed autistic at age 45

Sydney was diagnosed autistic at age 45 after living a traumatic and tumultuous life. This life included many menial jobs followed by a long period of homelessness. She grew up in England but moved to Wales for 20 years, finally moving back to marry the love of her life. She lives with her husband and enjoys reading, playing the guitar and knitting.

I HAVE ALWAYS LOVED music and was obsessed with certain bands when I was young. I would collect *all* their records (all formats) and every magazine with interviews in it, and go and see them live multiple times all over the country. I have calmed down a lot now and tend not to get so fired up about things, but I still love music and I play the guitar, working out other people's songs by ear.

I have an intense eye for detail and spotting mistakes and have been a proofreader. I am good at spotting patterns and how things connect. I have a very good memory, especially for numbers. I can be very determined, I am very loyal and I enjoy my own company. As an employee, I believe I am there to do the work and not chat with colleagues; I am a hard worker and take pride in working quickly and accurately. I am very independent and resourceful. I am good at problem-solving and thinking "outside the box".

Things I struggle with include making phone calls. Receiving them is not so bad, but still I sometimes can't think of what to say on the spot. Now I still struggle if I have to converse with anyone who is not my husband or one of our friends – I agonise afterwards over whether I have said what I needed to say, whether they understood me correctly, and whether I have understood them correctly. Could they have meant something else? Have I got it wrong? Have I said anything weird? I always struggled with all kinds of relationships, not understanding what I was doing wrong. Friends would just stop being friends with no explanation and often with a lot of hostility. I had to move house multiple times until I got my own space because of falling out with co-tenants. I found it impossible to keep a job because of falling out with bosses and co-workers.

I also have sensory issues. For example, when there is more than one person talking at once, I can't hear either of them. Also, listening when there is back-ground noise – I simply cannot hear what people are saying. If possible, I don't ever speak to anyone in shops, even to ask where something is, and I always use the self-checkout if available. So I hate going to shops with anyone. I struggle with bright lights, and I used to al-ways carry sunglasses until I got light-responsive lenses in my glasses. I struggle with smells and find cigarette smoke and some sharply scented perfumes particularly difficult to cope with. I can find clothing uncomfortable or scratchy, and I dress purely for comfort with no idea of style or appearance.

As a child, I was extremely precocious and quite strange. I read at a level far above my age group. I pre-ferred to spend time alone or with adults rather than other children. Occasionally, I became unable to speak when under extreme stress. I had terrible difficulty with toileting and had accidents even into my teenage years. I always seemed to have a different understand-ing of instructions that others seemed to easily follow. I felt different, and it seemed to me I was treated dif-ferently too. I was constantly bullied and picked on. I have always felt I had to abide by a different set of rules to everyone else.

Growing up as a supposedly "normal" person, masking was essential, and I think it likely I would have been put away if I hadn't! Every day, I have to mask to a certain extent, to be polite and acknowledge people. I mask every time I go out, every time I have to speak to someone. Times when I haven't masked are noteworthy. When I am very distressed, I am unable to speak and people's alarm around me at these times is remarkable – from being called "grumpy" to the extreme measure of having an ambulance called.

Aside from this, I had such tremendous social problems that I was forced to utterly retreat from society and hide in the middle of a wood. The reason I ended up in a tent in a wood is a fairly long process... I had always had trouble at all the many jobs I had – disciplinary meetings and constant criticism of my manner, my appearance, my mode of speech, and all aspect of relations with other staff. I kept changing job to get away, but, of course, the same thing kept on happening. I was always trying to think of ways to earn a living that didn't involve this kind of torture, but when you are right in the situation, it is very difficult to think clearly, and I couldn't see a way out. I had a lodger in my house as well as a boss at work who was determined to grind me to dust. This lodger had serious mental difficulties and severe alcoholism. So I had no respite at home either. It was a constant round of stress and torture.

I had what I assumed was a small breakdown but which I know now was autistic burnout, and got signed off work by the doctor. I used this time to think about what I could do. I knew that properties in Wales were so cheap that it might mean I could buy a house without needing a mortgage and would be able to afford to live only on the dole.* So I moved to Wales thinking I would get some peace and quiet and not have to work. Unfortunately, the dole office had different ideas and insisted I apply for hundreds of extremely unsuitable jobs, or they would stop my dole. Luckily, I am so bad at job interviews that I was safe for a while, but I did get a part-time job eventually. After a year, the same thing happened with the disciplinary proceedings because of the way I speak.

I was devastated and just wanted to give up. I had managed to save some money while working, so I went to New Zealand (Aotearoa) for six months, living out of a car and staying on extremely remote, isolated and usually deserted unmanned campsites far out in the middle of nowhere. Here, I had space and time to think again about what I could do to live my life without constantly

---

* Unemployment support payment.

being told that everything I did and said was wrong. All I could tell now was that I needed to be utterly alone and surrounded by nature.

I remembered that back home I had seen signs at the side of the roads sometimes saying "Woods for Sale", but I had never really thought about what that might mean. I looked up the two main wood-selling websites and found that they were not hugely expensive, and that if I sold my house, I would be able to buy one and probably have enough money to live on the interest. This was 2004, so even ordinary savings got 5 per cent a year!

So when I got home, I sold my house, bought a plot of woodland and a campervan to live in on it. All went well until the financial crash of 2008 when my income from interest dried up, and I had to sell the van as it was expensive to keep on the road. I managed to get hold of a 30- or 40-year-old leaky caravan to live in. It was necessary for the winters, but for the summers, I found a lovely clearing in the centre of the wood. I built a tiny shed to keep a gas stove and a few tins of food in, and pitched a tent to sleep in.

After four years, I found I was hurting my back folding myself in half to go through the doorway, so I thought long and hard about a better structure. It is not permitted to build anything permanent or that could conceivably be a dwelling, so I couldn't build a cabin as

I would have liked. I settled on a polytunnel as it was light and roomy, and easy to transport into the centre of the wood. I lived in that for four more years (I think – it's a bit hazy) until I got my diagnosis of autism and moved to a flat.

The only cure I have ever heard of for autistic burn-out is rest, peace and quiet, and total tranquillity. For me, it also involves being completely alone. Being in the centre of a wood with nobody knowing I was there, not having to speak to anyone, just communing with deer, squirrels, badgers, foxes, birds, and watching my trees grow, was the best therapy I could have had. It was immensely healing. I was able to fully recharge myself and I was at peace. It helped, massively!

My journey to autism diagnosis really began at age 36 when I finally had time to put my mind to finding out what was going wrong in my life and why. I sought an official diagnosis, but the doctor didn't know who to refer me to, and I believe there was no service for adult diagnosis at the time. At age 43, I was forced to return to the doctor with a bad abscess and she then referred me to the new service which had not long started up. Two years later, I got my diagnosis. It was a long drawn-out and difficult process, but I had done so much research that I knew without question that it was the diagnosis I needed.

After receiving the autism diagnosis, I was able to claim PIP (Personal Independence Payment, a disability allowance) and a small pension I had earned. I was able to rent a flat and move indoors. I connected with the online autistic community and made friends with people whom I understood and who understood me. I started to learn to accept myself and be accepted by others for the first time in my life. I was able to reassess everything that had happened to me in the light of a new understanding and began to see why those things had happened. This made me less angry at people who had mistreated me because I was able to understand, to some extent, what I had done to make them cross with me. I became a much calmer and more placid person, more at ease with myself and the world.

After I got diagnosed and moved to my flat, I got a part-time job with a learning disability charity. I wrote and designed an Autism Awareness and Acceptance Course which we presented to local police officers, social workers and others who may come into contact with autistic people in the course of their work. I was also asked to tell my life story at several conferences and functions, and I designed a slide show to illustrate it. The place I worked for didn't like it, but all the autistic people I have spoken to think it's brilliant, so I have been making it freely available.

Now that I have the diagnosis, I am much more aware of things I know I will not be able to do or will struggle with. I no longer try to converse verbally with neurotypicals as they rarely understand my meaning or I theirs. I have new friends because I moved to be with my now-husband. He has ADHD, and, in my opinion, all of his (now our) friends are neurodivergent to some degree – neurotypical people just don't get neurodivergent people and I think it would be unusual for neurotypical and neurodivergent people to mix voluntarily. In short, they all get me and accept me.

I can't help thinking that if I had had support at age 16, I could have continued with education and gained some qualifications. However, I feel that even with qualifications many autistic people face discrimination and are disadvantaged because of our social differences and fail to reach our full potential. Having been officially autistic may have prevented some of the workplace bullying I experienced, but given my latest employment, I'm not sure. They knew I was autistic (indeed, they had employed me as an autistic consultant), but they still gave me a hard time. But also, I wouldn't have done half of the mad things I have done, and I have done some mad stuff! The fact remains that when I was young in the 1970s and 1980s, it was widely believed that only boys were autistic, and there were set and stereotypical ways in which autism presented, which are very different to the ways female autism presents, so I understand why I was not diagnosed as a youngster. However, I do wonder why I was not diagnosed with anything other than attention-seeking behaviour and why nobody thought it was worth trying to help me or why I might be seeking attention. My family utterly reject my diagnosis and say that I'm just eccentric and quirky and always have been. People who have just met me say I'm nothing like some autistic boy they know of, or I seem to be communicating with them perfectly well. Autistic people just get it and accept me.

All autistic people are as individual as any people, and you cannot apply what you know about one autistic person you meet to the next. If you want to help an autistic person, you need to ask them about their needs and sensory sensitivities. Autistic people can be very blunt and often do not see the necessity (or have the energy) for trivial social niceties. It's very rare that we mean to be rude, and we are often mortified to be told that we are. If people understand this, and try not to judge when we slip up, it makes life a lot easier.

CHAPTER 6

Walk lightly on the earth

Zoë

Canada · Diagnosed autistic at age 44

Zoë is living in Toronto with their two dogs. Employed full-time, s'he enjoys art, hiking, camping, cycling and motorcycling when s'he has down time.

I TEND TO DO things alone as perhaps many autistics do. I completed, for example, a few solo motorcycle and backpacking trips. I think these are really exceptional experiences. From my experience, not a lot of autistics think they are capable of this stuff. I didn't know I was autistic, and I had no one telling me no. I was just like, what about this, because I had total freedom with no real guidance or support from family that was holding me down. It felt very empowering, I suppose.

As a child, I really always wanted to play piano, but

we couldn't afford it because my mother had got my sister and me a pony. I wasn't one to stand up for me, and I didn't want to disappoint her. You know, someone else might say, "I don't want this, I want this." But I didn't. And I had this pony, it was an expectation, so I rode horses as a child. But it's stupid because only really the wealthy can truly afford that lifestyle: to show, and to have a trailer, and to have all the gear. It's ridiculous that I even had a pony, but I did. It made me very physically strong, though.

I do remember almost nothing of my childhood. I have some fleeting memories. Mostly stressful or frightening ones. I remember my father pushing my mother into some furniture. I remember my mother was late one night, and my father said, "Your mother is dead." This is what I remember from childhood. So, you know, later on I'm just traumatised. I tell myself, there's nothing wrong with me, I've just experienced trauma. But at some point in my 30s, I realised no, this is more than childhood trauma. There is something else here that's not the trauma.

My dad is from India, so I'm half Indian, so when I was a child, I knew I was different. But why am I different? Am I different because I'm half Indian? Am I different because I went to a Catholic school and I've never been baptised? My mother just thought it was a better education. Am I different because I've moved so many times? You know, I knew I was different. I didn't know why. My assumption was that it was all other reasons. I remember thinking I was different but I couldn't place it.

In high school, I read *The Chrysalids*,* and when I read it, my mind went "bing". There are more of us out there. Now, looking back, I'm like, that was it. There are other people that are on the same wavelength, that are like us. But I didn't know what it was. Now I'm like, yeah, that's the autism. That's not what the Chrysalids are, but for me that was the connection I made.

Autistic signs and traits were missed when I was growing up. My mom said I didn't speak until I was two. I used to spin in circles; I loved to be out in the grass and just spinning and spinning and spinning. That was the best. I was also very shy. They told me I was extraordinarily shy. I remember that. I was so scared to speak. But was it that I was scared or was it that I was selectively mute because I couldn't find the words in my jumble of thoughts? There was so much going on. Am I mute or is it that I just can't find the right answers in this chaos? But they did consider me very shy.

My family wasn't the healthiest family. We didn't

---

* *The Chrysalids* is a science fiction novel by John Wyndham.

go out much. We weren't allowed out. We didn't have friends over, we didn't go to other people's houses, so I have no experience of what other families are like. I have no experience of people with good relationships, and, of course, I wasn't invited places because I wasn't that kind of kid. I remember one of my friends, later, she was like, "My dad doesn't like you." And now I'm like, it's because of the autism. I was too weird for her dad. So that was something. How do you become safe as an autistic child when home is unsafe? You don't. There was so much going on in my life, you know. There was absolutely trauma and some degree of neglect, but my mother did her best to protect us.

I was very artistic through high school. It was always my favourite class. But it was the class the teachers would always take away if they wanted to punish the whole class. It was brutal for people like me. But I did art and I changed schools a lot. It was all disjointed. But I did it through high school. In high school, by which time my mom had left my dad and she was a single mom and we moved a lot. She'd run out of money, and she'd be like, "You've got to go figure things out on your own again." This happened three or four times when I was in high school. So when I was finishing high school, I was homeless again. I didn't have anywhere to keep things, to have an art portfolio. I didn't have anywhere to work.

I didn't have my own space. So I couldn't put together a portfolio to apply to art school, and I didn't feel safe talking about that with the adults, so I did a biology degree instead. I thought maybe this is a better solution for me. Which is kind of brutal. I'm serious; I failed my way through the maths in my science degree. But I did do a fine art minor, and I did very, very well. I even sold my artwork in university. But I haven't really drawn since. I didn't want to be a starving artist. I probably wouldn't have been, given that I was selling art as a university student, you know, but that didn't get into my little brain.

I think that if I had got my diagnosis sometime during university, I would have been better off because at university I started to sense that I was different, that when I would do things, people would respond by glancing at each other. Obviously, they were looking over my head, saying she's just done a faux pas, and I'm like, "What have I done? What did I do again?" I could almost picture what people look like when they were looking at me. They were rolling their eyes, or they were looking over my head, giving each other glances. This is the experience of being autistic. If you don't know you're autistic, people are going to be questioning everything you are doing, and you are not going to understand what it is that you are doing wrong.

I almost wish I could capture these faces. I used to be a very prolific photographer. Starting at the age of 14, it was one of the things I did – as an outsider looking in. I would take pictures of things because I wasn't part of the group, so I was capturing the group. I have a picture of this woman I went on a camping trip with, with some other friends, and she saw me taking pictures. She just made this monkey action, and I've got this picture of her acting like a monkey and giving this monkey face to me. I realise, looking back now, that was her making fun of me, do you know? People are like, "Look at this weirdo."

After university, I didn't know what to do, but I wanted to work and to travel, so I went to Korea. In 1998, I worked for a year, then I left Korea to backpack. I took the slow boat to China, and I travelled China by myself. I spent two weeks in Beijing and just went where I could. I had my *Lonely Planet*, and I learned simple Chinese. I speak some Korean because I spent a year there, travelling by myself in Korea. So my Korean's okay, although it has been 20 years, so I'm not going to say it's okay any more, but I can read it, you know. I also studied intensively at a university language institute while I was there, but still it was 20 years ago. So in China, I picked up some Chinese, like I can do this, I can barter in the market and I can travel around. Amazing. Then

Vietnam. That's where I was for Y2K.* Then back up and into Laos and Thailand, and then I went into Cambodia briefly with a friend from university.

I got to Bangkok, then I flew to Istanbul for a week and London for a week, and back into Canada. And then I just kept going west until I got back to Korea again, and I did four more years in Korea. Different jobs. Meeting amazing people. When I finally came back to Canada, that's when I really stood out like a sore thumb. Because when I was in Korea, I didn't stand out any more than any foreigner is going to stand out. The foreigners who go to Korea, they are not the most normal people. They are really unusual for a variety of reasons. When I came back from Korea, I certainly noticed that I wasn't connecting with women. I've never connected with women. They would almost shame or ostracise me for being me.

I didn't marry until I was in my 40s, and I felt safe with my husband, someone I trusted given that I didn't feel safe with a lot of people. And certainly I am not safe with men. I didn't realise I was autistic. I didn't understand what I was struggling with, and I entered this relationship and then all hell broke loose for me personally, and, of course, it affected the relationship. Honestly, by the time I was 42 and realised I was autistic, and at

---

* Year 2000.

44 getting a diagnosis, I had done a lot of my own masking, figuring out how to hide the autism for many years. So, of course, when I tell people, "Hey, I found this out, this is true for me," they are like, "I don't see it. I don't believe you. That's not true." Which honestly put me into more isolation that I was before. But those who knew me when I was a child or into my 20s believe it because they knew me before the mask was complete.

Then you add into that some of the meltdowns that happened as a result of not being seen, not being heard, and that's a huge part of what happened in my marriage. I didn't know what was happening, he didn't know what was happening, and nobody believed me. I had a professional, very, very thorough diagnosis. I mean, I had two full-on days of assessments. I had two six-hour days of testing, plus all of these multiple-choice questionnaires and all these things in advance that I did, that my husband did, my mother did, so it was exceptionally thorough, my assessment. And yet people are still going, "I don't believe you. I don't see it. I don't know what you're talking about." I'm like, "Are you kidding me?"

I was so excited to learn about autism, but really it has turned my life upside down and not for the best. I lost my friends, my marriage fell apart, and I wasn't able to advocate for myself, even in my current job. My husband and I are separating right now, and I will say that possibly has a fair amount to do with me not realising I was autistic until we had married. And all of the trauma that unleashed in our relationship. I'm not quite sure if this is permanent. He feels it is, but I committed to a lifetime partnership.

I haven't got a support network in place – not a good one. I met a woman who practises some type of black magic. I saw her yesterday, and she had so much insight for my experience right now. I also talked to my friend who is a much older gentleman – he's in his 80s and he is a doctor in social work. He is like, "You need to check yourself into the mental hospital. You need to get out of your home, you need to get away from your job, it's not good for you." The Western medicine says you've got a big problem, the alternative medicine says you've got a big problem: oh shit, I've got a big problem.

I work full-time. I have the most exhausting job in social work, in homelessness, in a shelter. My job is not good for me. It would not be good for a regular person. I've been there one year and that was my goal. I just feel like I can't do it any more. Also, I've needed an assistant or a team for a long time, and the employer hasn't been willing to give me one. I'm just so burnt out. So burnt out. This is the kind of job that only someone like me could do. I don't panic in a work crisis, and there are many, but it's not to say it isn't taking a toll.

I struggle with interpersonal connections and networking. This makes finding employment challenging. That was always really true for me, and I never figured out what it was. Recognising that for whatever reason people are quickly turned off by me. So that ends up being a weakness. It's not even something I can control, but as a result I have some social phobia. It developed because I didn't know why this was happening. So while I am seen as very outgoing and gregarious, it exhausts me and I do need my downtime, but I think the weakness is that even though I am outgoing and gregarious, people don't necessarily want to be around me. Right now, I haven't been socialising much at all. I really enjoyed being with my husband because he was so outgoing and gregarious. We were a really good socialising team. We'd go out, we'd socialise, we'd host events too, and it worked out really well. But I'm not now because I don't have a safety net; I'm not just going to go out alone any more.

I no longer trust people to respond nicely to me. And if I do share about my autism, I don't trust that they are going to hold that in a safe way. Absolutely not. I even told my mother and she said, "You're not autistic, I don't believe it." And probably because I said, "If I'm autistic, you're probably autistic too, Mom," she's like, "I don't believe it."

There was this one episode where we went to a friend's place and I told my husband before we went that I can handle two hours. I can socialise for two hours. And then we went out on her balcony and it got dark; dusk fell and there are bright lights in the parking lot, and it's dark and bright lights. So it's this thing with extreme contrast which I have learned I can't handle. It's very triggering and overwhelming. Then I told that friend about the autism diagnosis and she says, "Really, I don't see it. I don't see it." And so I got pretty upset. I had a bit of a meltdown. I'm like, "I need out, I need to go." So it was this combination of being there too long, dealing with the bright lights and then her challenging me that she doesn't believe my assessment. This led to a conflict with my husband as well, since he believed my autistic meltdown was inappropriate although I was unable to control it.

One of the other reasons I don't share about my autism diagnosis is because when I realised that I was autistic in 2014, Asperger's was still a diagnosis. But after that, it was included under autism, and since there are autistic kids that are non-speaking with other developmental disabilities, if you say to someone, "I am autistic," they are like, "You are not autistic, you are not like my disabled nephew." So that is challenging. Personally, I wish that Asperger's wasn't dropped, because I cannot realistically go out and tell people I am autistic because their understanding of autism is profoundly disabled young white boys.

You have got to believe me that this is real. I would like people to know that autism looks different from how most people think it does, and it absolutely looks different in women and girls, especially older individuals, much older, who have learned to cope and mask for decades even. I would like them to understand that autism is a series of anomalies in neurological processing. Sometimes it is strengths, sometimes it is deficits. I would love to be explicit to show people that someone cannot just be a little bit autistic because they love patterns or don't like tapioca. It is also amazing strength. Pattern recognition, out-of-the-box thinking, artistic ability, in addition to the sensitivities and challenges.

Things that are not human or on a natural scale are not good for autistic individuals. Giant buildings, concrete towers, sounds cascading around us with no green space. Nothing to soften the environment. It's actually killing us and quite plausibly making people more symptomatic because there are less things to soften the sounds. Don't take this the wrong way, but I think that we all have a need for nature, and if we don't have that, we might get suddenly overwhelmed by the world around us. We were not born into a concrete jungle field with sirens and screaming people. Years ago, Indigenous people used to walk lightly on the earth and teach their kids to walk lightly on the earth and be with nature. Today's kids run around screaming and playing with plastic toys. We created a world that's killing the world and we are so less connected. I think it is overwhelming for autistic people, but it is overwhelming for the natural world and anything that is connected to nature in any way. As biological organisms that come from the earth, we have, and need to have, that connection.

CHAPTER 7

The penny drops

Elizabeth

Australia · Diagnosed autistic at age 70

Elizabeth was born in 1947 in a country town, and she was diagnosed autistic in 2017. She describes her life as "varying between a three-ring circus and a total train wreck, with times when the train wreck happened inside the circus".

NEUROTYPICAL PEOPLE HAVE stories. In general, a story will have a beginning, a middle and an end. Ours tend to have a beginning, and then you get partway toward the middle and then you launch off on some tangent or long-winded explanation, and then you start thinking okay, that wasn't the answer to the question which was asked, so you go back and try to pick it up. And if you ever do get to the end of the story, three hours later, you've completely forgotten...

I talk too much. It's the sort of stuff that people

complain about. I don't get to the point, which is pretty common because what you are generally trying to do is to make sure that people understand what it is that you are getting at because they, neurotypicals, pick up subtle clues which you don't, and so you feel that you need to go into detail or explain a lot. So you keep explaining it to make sure you're satisfied that they've understood what you are on about. They have long since given up listening to this diatribe, and half the time you get interrupted before you are anywhere near the end of it. And it's the sort of stuff, particularly with job interviews where you are answering questions, or seminars, they just groan or roll their eyes, and go, "Oh, here we go again..."

Eventually, the penny drops. You don't know why, but it dawns on you that you've either got to be more succinct or more to the point. You just try not to put yourself in a situation where that's going to happen. And again, this is all because you don't know. It's these sorts of things, that is why it is such a relief to realise that being autistic is a manifestation or ability or a different way of explaining, so you don't steer clear of those situations so much because you think, "Right, I've just got to make sure that I get to the point in this much space, not this much space." Someone can say something, and you suddenly see 27 ramifications. They don't want that many; they want two or three or half a dozen or a broad overview, without all the detail. Once you become aware of this, you've got to remember to try to get to the point. If you do leave out something, presumably they will stick up their hand and ask, "What do you mean by that?" And then you've got permission to expand or go into more detail. But again, you don't know why this has happened. You just somehow know that that's how I am, and it works better if I keep a bit of a lid on it, or if I don't get myself into a situation where it's likely to happen. With a lot of this stuff, it would have been really nice if someone had said, this is part of this constellation of things, and you just need to be careful about that, and neurotypicals see these sort of thing, and it's all tied up with the social stuff and you don't read the social signs and so forth. It comes out as one of the differences between neurotypical and neurodivergent people.

I grew up in a country town where groups of girls went around together and all went to the dance on Saturday night or went down to the pool together, and I was always on the outer. I was academically able. I had been christened the walking encyclopaedia by all and sundry when I was partway through state school,* and

---

* Primary or elementary school.

I was never part of any groups. It was a double-edged sword. It would have been nice to go out sometimes and have a group of friends, but then if I ever did get close to any of them, all they talked about was make-up and dresses and shoes and hairdos. I'm not interested in these things! I was looking for other people like me, but there weren't any. So you learned to live with being on your own.

Thinking back, I knew I was different as far back as pre-school. You see the arguments like, "Should I tell my children about their autism diagnosis? I don't want them to feel different or be labelled," and you think, "For crying out loud, just do it!" They might feel different? Well, hello, you'll find they already probably do, if you bothered to talk to them. I mean, for me, I sometimes wanted to be part of a group, and have the group as friends, but on the other hand, they manifestly didn't want me as part of the group, or as an individual's friend. Even though autistic people are not supposed to pick up well on social clues and language, that much was pretty obvious!

As an adult, I had this situation where I had left the marital home. I couldn't handle the responsibilities of the kids and running the house with no support, and trying to work as well. The marriage had fallen to pieces anyway. So I moved out. The older kid was already seen to be gifted and lived in his own world, and was only apparently worried about whether I'd still come back at weekends and cook his favourite meal! And the other one had wildly oscillating reactions, from "How could you?" to "Thank goodness you're out of our lives" and all points in between.

I used to go "home" at weekends, mainly to do the washing for the kids, and make sure the house hadn't burnt or fallen down, and make vague attempts to keep the kids roughly under control. Masking, biting my tongue, anxiety and depression levels sky-rocketing, life was hell on wheels, except the wheels had mostly fallen off.

When the kids were 14 and 15, I was living in a residential college at one of the universities, running the library. I was also doing tutorials on how to research and how to distinguish rubbish websites from real websites, and teaching postgrads how to do bibliographies and how to cite websites and all that sort of stuff, and this particular day one of the kids rang up and said, "Oh, we got home from school and Dad's on the bathroom floor and we can't wake him up and we've rung the ambos* already and we thought we had better ring you." Anyway, they had come home from school and basically

---

* Ambulance.

found him dead on the bathroom floor! When your kids are 14 or 15, it made for a pretty fancy year that year. I had to move out on the spot from where I was and move back in with them. And some people had said, "You know, you've probably got PTSD from that." And I said, "No, my life was a train wreck *way* before that happened." It obviously didn't help, but it was just another brick on the top of this teetering wall which just made it a little bit more wobbly than it already was.

Fifteen months later, my mother became terminally ill, and the following six months were also fraught, of course, and it was after all that when I just couldn't keep up any hope of trying to go to work in among all the rest of it. More burnout, except I had to keep going...so more doctors, psychiatrists, pills and resigning from work, which turned out to be forever, and on to the disability pension where I stayed until the government automatically shifted me to the old age pension when I was old enough.

Leading up to my autism diagnosis, there was this article on women who don't know they are autistic, and I started scanning it because it was the third article down on that particular day, and, "Hello," I suddenly thought, "That's it!" It's not that I'm crackers, it's not that I wasn't brought up properly, it's not that I've got depression and anxiety – yes, I have, but they are symptoms rather than the causes – it's not any one of two dozen things. I had been saying that to the shrink* for I don't know how long, and I'd been diagnosed with all the usual stuff: depression and anxiety, with bipolar, with borderline personality disorder, and a string of these other strange mental health diagnoses. And none of them ever really quite fit, or explained much. They all explained a bit but none of them explained *all* of it.

And it was around about the same time that the offspring living far away had said they had found this group of people, or the group had found them, and has anybody thought about autism? And then around about the same time was when the ex-daughter-in-law asked whether there is anyone in the family with autism because the kids' schools are asking about it. And I'd already been seeing a GP** and a shrink for depression and anxiety which was horrendous to the extent that half the time I couldn't function. The depression was ghastly, and earlier in my life there had been several "nervous breakdowns". There were all those sorts of things happening where I found all this stuff and carted some of it off to the GP. I already had a mental health plan anyway because of the depression and anxiety, and I said, "What do you reckon about this?" The GP kept

---

* Psychiatrist.
** General Practitioner, medical doctor.

saying, "I think you are bipolar," and I said, "No, I don't think I am. If I get a high, it lasts only about ten minutes, not weeks." And the GP and the shrink are continually saying, "Maybe you should take these pills," but nothing ever properly worked. I said, "I've done a lot of chasing around and found this woman who deals with adult females who are thought to be on the spectrum." That was difficult enough as it was because there aren't too many psychologists working in that area, and the GP finally told me to go and see her.

So anyway, I also went back to the old GP we used to see in the city, and told him about the article and my research and that the country GP had referred me to a psychologist, and he said, "I suppose that fits better than anything else, doesn't it?" I said, "Indeed it does." So it was that constellation of all those things, and it all happened in the space of three to six months in between waiting for appointments and that sort of thing. While I was waiting for the appointment with the psychologist for the assessment, that's when I got on to the internet and got on to the library and did a pile of research and reading and looking back at past events. I was well prepared. Before I went to see her, I was quite sure that I was on the spectrum, or Asperger's, and hoped that she would just confirm that.

I only had a single one-hour interview for the assessment as I couldn't afford the full assessment. The psychologist had sent me some questionnaires to fill in before this interview, and I realised that the first one was exactly the same, although set out differently, as the ASQ* online questionnaire which my research had previously discovered. I have chronically scored between 40 and 45 on this, depending on whether I answer as now, or as I can best remember from when I was a teenager at high school – maybe somewhere between ages 14 and 17. This indicated that there was no doubt that I was on the spectrum.

At the assessment, the psychologist and I, we'd just been casually chatting, and she let me ramble on, and when I looked at the clock and said what do you reckon, and she just looked at me and said, "Oh my god," nearly fell off her chair laughing and said, "Is the Pope a Catholic? Why are you here at all? Of course you are." And that stage, I said, "Right, we'll leave it at that, thanks." There was no point at that stage in me going through the full diagnostic procedure as they were talking about $2000 or $3000 and I'm on the old age pension. The lack of support is difficult enough for those who are kids, teenagers or young adults, let alone older people! As I said to somebody recently, the whole of my life has

---

* Autism Spectrum Quotient.

been a tragic-comedic train wreck, so I can live with the rest of it, however much longer there is. But there's all the other stuff with the offspring and the grandchildren and all the rest. So I thought, the sooner I can get something out of some medical person or psych to say that, yes, I am on the spectrum, or I'm Asperger's, or whatever it happens to be, at least that's more grist to their mill and that's about the best that I can do to help. I'm quite happy with where I am (well, as far as one can be happy with the disasters), and there's not much more I can do. I'm certainly not going to be looking to NDIS,* which isn't available after you reach pension age anyway (which is scandalous as they force you to use My Aged Care which is complicated and doesn't provide anything remotely approaching the support that NDIS does), or getting any further support or anything like that.

After I had done a lot of reading (as I said I tend to go overboard with whatever I do), I did a pile of research and all the rest of it, and discovered a whole bundle of small symptoms that, when you add them up, makes a whole constellation of stuff. With things like the barbed-wire labels on the back of your neck. And the family used to say, "What's the problem with them?" And the

---

* National Disability Insurance Scheme.

bright lights and flickering fluorescents which no one else can see, and which drove me silly. And there's been a handful of those sorts of things we sort of look at and you think, right, that one fits. It's not me being cranky or me being "What's wrong with you, or how can you think like that when nobody else does?" When I got to that stage in my life when I had the diagnosis, it was such a relief to finally have an explanation that actually fitted all of these stray bits and pieces. For example, my child and I are both photosensitive. People used to say, "Why do you live in a bloody cave? Turn the light on, put the blinds up. Why do you always have to have your sunglasses to go down the street?" It's all those little niggly things that helped all the bits fall into place.

A lot of this stuff had manifested as a child and teenager, and I have just been living with it ever since. It's about bloody time somebody found out about all of this stuff. I had been that way since the 1950s or 1960s. It was confirmation and, for once, nobody had said when I was doing this research that you are barking up the wrong tree or you've gone out on this branch when you should have gone out on that branch, or that it's all very interesting but that's not you. I mean I had chased up all of this stuff and done all of this research, and the more I did, the more I was convinced that it's not just me, but probably my brother and mother, certainly the kids, possibly the grandkids, not to mention some cousins and other rellies* are on the spectrum.

I don't know that it would have helped to know my autism diagnosis earlier because of how old I was when it would have happened. How much support and knowledge were there in a country town in the 1950s, 1960s and 1970s? But I was academically able too, so that covered up a whole lot of other things. So what sort of stuff at school would have happened, I don't know. There weren't even any school counsellors or anything like that when I went through primary and high school. Somebody like a local church minister might step in if somebody's father got killed in a farm accident or somebody's mother or sibling died, but a lot of blokes did die of heart attacks or farm accidents. It wasn't an unusual situation. And I'm not sure it would have made a great deal of difference at the time, because the sort of stuff that is available these days in the education system wasn't available back then.

It probably would have been useful to know I was autistic when I was working 30 or 40 years ago, where you tend to get so involved and then burn yourself out and have "nervous breakdowns". Or get depressed and you didn't know it was depression, but you knew you didn't

---

* Relatives.

want to be there. And one of the ways I got around that, until everything totally fell to pieces, was the last job I had for quite a considerable time where I was actually running a one-person library. There were other people in the organisation, like admin and teaching staff, but I only saw them at lunchtime and morning teatime or when they came down to the library. Basically, the students came and went, and I wasn't actually working closely with anybody else all day. That meant that I could have the lights in my office how I wanted them, and I didn't have somebody else saying whatever. So working on my own was an answer to a problem. And again, probably if there had been people who were not pushing you too far or not overloading you, I might have stayed in the mainstream longer than I did.

My first diagnosed "nervous breakdown" was when I was 22 and my first marriage was a disintegrating disaster. Fortunately, there were no kids, so I just moved back to the city, got a good job, lived alone and carried on. Hardly anyone had heard of Asperger's or autism back then, and certainly not in adult females! The second "nervous breakdown" was 1982, shortly prior to the second marriage. Ten weeks off work with that one. Luckily, I had a sympathetic boss who, I discovered later, when I ran out of sick leave, had not bothered to tell staffing and the pay office that I was still away. There used to be nice people in the world back then, and if your work was valued, you got some recognition. However, that year had been hellish at work too. We had been forcibly amalgamated with several other similar institutions and part of our place was to be hived off and the whole establishment was rejigged. We all had to re-apply for our own jobs or other similar positions, and I then spent half the year sitting on interview panels interviewing people who had worked for me for jobs they were already doing, or for jobs they didn't want because there weren't enough new positions at their classification to go round existing staff. Ghastly business! It was that job I took maternity leave from for the first kid and then resigned from after the second kid. I'd been there about 11 years.

As you've doubtless picked up, a lot of autistic people don't have a huge quantity of friends and those there are tend to be serial. You know, you have a friend for a while and then they disappear out of your life, and then you pick up somebody else and five, ten, whatever years later, they disappear. But anyway, the people that I know reasonably well now are contacts I have picked up through social media or where I'm living and even back to high school and all points in between. I mean I've basically come out to them as autistic, and I don't think anybody vanished off the face of the earth as a result. A couple of people have just rolled their eyes and said, "Okay we knew you were gaga anyway," or "If you want to stick a label on it, that's fine, but we'll still talk to you on Facebook and we know you're mad anyway, so it doesn't make any difference." And a couple of others have said, "Ahh, right, that explains a whole lot of stuff," and it turns out that those people are either in the same boat or they've been diagnosed with something like PTSD or ADHD. But when we get together, we find that we've got a handful of autism things here, a lot of common things (often ADHD things) and then a couple of PTSD things over here. We find that there is a big lump of common stuff in the middle. While they've got one diagnosis and I've got another, we've got far more in common than we have in differences.

CHAPTER 8

Neurotypes

Rose

England · Diagnosed autistic at age 58

Rose was diagnosed autistic five years ago and spends far
too much time on Twitter* but is unrepentant about this
given the many positive outcomes that have resulted from
it, including finding neurokin, getting involved in autism research and being part of this book.

WHEN I WAS 18 and I was at university, I was situa-
tionally non-speaking. I literally couldn't speak in a lot
of study situations. And I didn't even know that this
was a thing. When we graduated, I remember being at
the noticeboard looking at the results and somebody
said "Who is that?" because I got a first-class honours

---

* Twitter is now known as X.

degree. And somebody said, "Oh, she's the one who just smiles and never speaks." Well, that was me. I thought I was very shy, but that didn't really work because there were certain situations where I could speak up. I would actually take a stand on things.

The weird thing when I was in my early 30s, when I worked in the probation service, I was going for a lot of audiology tests, and the audiology people said I should be able to hear better than I could. I went back to the probation service, and we had a psychologist there who was attached to the unit working with the offenders looking at the psychological underlying basis for their offending, and I was saying to her, "It is really mystifying because I literally can't hear things, but the audiology people are telling me that I should be able to." And she said, "It's probably something cognitive." That didn't make any kind of sense to me because I had an IQ that was way up there, so I was like, "I don't have any cognitive issues, you know." I was hyperlexic as a child, I was ahead on all my milestones, I was never behind on any developmental milestones. To my generation, autism was always strongly associated with delay.

Looking back and recognising autistic traits, I had these episodes that I would now see very clearly as meltdowns. Three massive ones. One when I was 15, one when I was in my 30s, and one when I was in my 50s.

In my family, when I was 15, I was doing mock exams, so that was part of it. I was at a very high-achieving girls' school. I had been given a free-place scholarship at the age of 11 because I got this astonishing mark in my 11-plus exam. I was under huge pressure, and I was in a very unfamiliar environment. None of the children I went to primary school with were at this school. Only one, who was a bully I really feared and didn't get on with. When I was 15, I remember being at home with my mum and I don't know what happened, but it was like an eruption, you know, a complete thing. And I remember being in the breakfast room and getting this chair and I was just banging the chair on the floor and later there were still dents on the wooden floor where I banged this chair. And it was like this massive release of pent-up energy, and I had this overwhelming urge to break or destroy something. But it's funny, because in meltdown I'll get this overwhelming urge, but I don't want to break something that matters or hurt anybody, so I went into the kitchen and got a big pack of eggs, and I went into the garden and I threw these eggs at the back of the house. And it was amazing because they smashed, and they were all dribbling down the back of the house. The bad thing about this was the egg stains never really went away. So, when I was 18 and I would bring a boy home, my parents would trundle them out into the garden and say, "Oh look, do you see up there? That's when she threw all these eggs."

But the funny thing is, there was this patch in my grandparents' house on the wall, a greasy patch that you could see through the paint that never went away. That was when my grandfather threw a pat of butter at the wall. And my mother, I remember distinctly as a child, we were having supper one night and she lost it, and she took a plate of spaghetti bolognese, and there was an airing thing with some sheets on it in the kitchen, and she threw the spaghetti bolognese and it was all sliding down these sheets. And just at that moment a neighbour popped in. I remember us all sitting there around the table having our meal and the neighbour there and the spaghetti sliding down the thing. The British thing of nobody saying anything, pretending nothing had happened.

The things about me just seemed to be like family traits, if you know what I mean. If you had talked to me about my outbursts, I would have said, "Well, my mum had those." She had another one in which she threw all our Christmas presents down the stairs. This was something I witnessed in my parents and my grandparents. It didn't seem that unusual to me, and that may be the case for a lot of autistic people who are growing up in neurodivergent families with neurodivergent ancestors, and we seem to be in the family mould. And it's only when we go outside our own family that we start to feel really different.

I suppose the precipitating factor in pursuing a diagnosis was I went to my GP after yet another problem at work. The problems at work would centre around some kind of dishonesty, bullying or abuse. Not necessarily at me. I didn't have to be directly involved in it, but when I became aware that things were happening that shouldn't be happening, I would try to raise it with senior management and they wouldn't do anything. I had to resign because I couldn't be part of it.

I think I went to my GP and said, "Look, to be absolutely frank with you, I am here yet again telling you that I have been bullied at work. This just keeps happening. Whatever job I'm in, something always ends up happening that causes me some moral discomfort." And I said to her, "I really think, quite honestly, I'm the only common denominator in all of these situations. I'm not saying it's my fault, but it has to have something to do with my psychology. Because if it has nothing to do with me, then why does it keep happening in every situation that I'm ever in?" And I said, "If I change jobs I just know it's going to happen again. It might take a week, it might take a month, it might take a year, but I know with this dreadful certainty that it will happen. And I just can't keep going through this. I need to know why."

When I went for my initial consultation about autism, I had an open mind. I'd been a mental health social worker, so obviously I had worked with people with depression, anxiety and personality disorder. It was difficult because I knew I hadn't got typical anxiety, typical depression. I didn't think I had what would be known as a personality disorder because, for example, I had very, very good attachment to my parents, a very loving home, no major childhood traumas. I had very functional and quite long-standing relationships, loving relationships, so I didn't fit the mould of somebody who had a very difficult early life which might have explained some of the later problems. But I couldn't even get to the point where I said, "I think I am autistic," because my GP was like, "Well, let's look at the first thing on your list." And I had written a kind of rationale for X, Y and Z equals I must be autistic, but we never got to that point. And to be frank, I gave up going through the medical system and I went off on my own. I spoke to a specialist service for women, and they couldn't assess me because I was outside their geographical catchment area, but this lovely woman spent an hour on the phone with me one lunchtime when I basically just sobbed down the phone, telling her stuff randomly, and she just said, "I think you should get assessed for autism. I really think you should get assessed for autism. Please try to get assessed for autism."

And that was enough to make me think, "Well, she's an expert in autism and she thinks I should get assessed," and then it was really lucky because I did some more research and found an autism assessment service nearby. They did an initial one-and-a-half-hour session which would determine if a full autism assessment was appropriate. And that only cost £150 and that was the key for me. Because I think at that stage it would have been really difficult to spend £1200 on a speculative autism assessment, but being able to go for a £150 meeting and then saying, "Yes, we do think you should have a full autism assessment," that gave me confidence that I'm not wasting anybody's time here.

Another primary reason I have got assessed at the age of nearly 59 was because I didn't want to become my mother. That was one reason. My mother became very anxious as she got over 70. I attribute a lot of that to being undiagnosed as autistic and to do with things like sensory overwhelm and not knowing why she is overwhelmed. She doesn't feel there is any reason why she needs to adjust her socialising or her environment or anything else, or give herself extra care. She spent her life looking after other people and not looking after herself because she somehow doesn't feel entitled, and I just thought I don't want to become like my mother.

And the other thing I thought about was my biggest dread of being parked in a residential care home for old people. You know the kind where you sit around the edge in chairs and there is a lot of gossip, and they bring in musicians who play raucous music. It's always music from the 1940s; however young you are, you always get Vera Lynn and it's just weird. And I've worked in places like that. And the smells, and the food, and the noise, and just everything about them. So I thought my best chance of escaping that fate – those two fates really – was to get diagnosed and to see if I might be autistic, and then to be able to say, "I am autistic and I need X, Y, Z." I think certainly in some medical situations now, I've been able to get some accommodations. Even if I can't get accommodations, I get treated marginally better by my GP practice now. I've been sort of advocating for about three years, and they must've had some training recently because they have suddenly become a lot nicer.

So that was what happened. But looking back, obviously the amazing thing about when you get your diagnosis is that you start tracking back and every day something comes to mind when I think, "Oh, of course." It's hard work because the older you are when you get your diagnosis, the more years of stuff you've got to track back through, and yet the less the mental health system and the autism support system seems to be interested in your outcomes because you are getting to the point where you won't have to work much longer. And I hear a lot of people say, even about themselves, is it worth getting a diagnosis at 70, 75?

There are the issues of ageing, and then there's gender. I mean, I really don't get along well with stuff that is geared towards women, not at all. I think that for me as a child, I quickly rejected the notion of being female because all the interesting jobs I saw were done by men and I didn't want to be limited. So I adopted the name of Jack, which I preferred to be known by because I didn't know any women builders, and I loved mixing cement and building stuff. And then when I was a late teen, I started wearing men's clothes. I really loved men's jackets and waistcoats and shirts and ties. I loved the whole thing of tying a tie and I just loved the big pockets, and I thought men's clothes were far more functional.

I got a very odd reaction to wearing men's clothes. If I was that age now, it wouldn't be an issue. I think that it is a really, really fascinating thing, because within the community of people who define themselves as autistic, there are far more non-binary people, far more LGBTQIA+ people. It's striking, and, oddly enough, that is where I found my social home as a teenager. I started working in the cinema in my late teens as a holiday job, and I went back every holiday through to university. In the cinema, it is predominantly gay, and we were all misfits – a couple of recovering heroin addicts, one was a museum curator, and the other was doing a PhD – and the manager employed us because the manager had one lung and he had been turned down for a lot of jobs because of the fact he had one lung. And when we looked around at the cinema staff, in our own way we were all people who struggled to find a place anywhere else, but this manager, he just said yes to all the people that everybody else said no to. And it was fabulous because we used to work till 11 o'clock at night, and then we'd go out and sit in the park and start talking about philosophy, and go back to someone's flat. I also went to a gay nightclub. I remember my parents, I was only 18, and I remember phoning home and saying we're going to the club. My dad, of course, being a police officer at that time, he knew the reputation of the place. He was like, "What!" And I just put the phone down quick. It was good because I just felt so at home with this group of people. I wasn't gay or bisexual. I was straight, but I just felt so comfortable with them because they were so non-judgemental and they were just good people, a lot of them, you know. And even now, when I am with a predominantly neurodivergent group of people, it is just so much more comfortable for me. I have to remind myself that that's what the allistic population gets most of the time. Most of the time, they are in situations where they are in a majority allistic group, and they feel the same comfort, and I have never known that. So, it's kind of bittersweet really because it makes you realise what you missed.

Also, I'm not keen on this idea where people say there is a female presentation of autism that is different from a male presentation. I've got male autistic friends who would have that more allegedly female presentation, and I have women friends who would have more obviously stereotypically male presentation. I don't think the presentation of being autistic is divided along gender lines.

I think the whole gender construction is fascinating. Personally, I am veering more towards not presenting as stereotypically female, not worrying about it because I think there is a lot of pressure on women which somewhat bypassed me, because there are a lot of things, I realised with hindsight, that I was supposed to know and do as a woman, that I didn't. I don't know whether it is because I didn't have girl friends, so I didn't have a group of women who were telling me how we were supposed to do this or how we were supposed to do that. So I was remarkably ignorant really of some of the trends about how you are supposed to maintain your body, how you are supposed to present your body. It just seemed nonsense to me. I think if I wasn't in a marriage with a man, I'd probably come out as non-binary, but I think it would be difficult for him. The poor man, he's been through enough. Since we've been married, he's had to cope with my realisation that I am autistic and taking on this autistic identity. I think to go down the route of saying, "Do you know what, I actually feel that I want to be a they/them rather than a she/her," it might be a step too far. I think eventually, if I end up on my own, then I will become that kind of person. And I adore non-binary people.

So going back, yes, I do wish, if I could have brought myself forward to the present day, that I would have known earlier about being autistic, but actually, historically, I think it would have been awful. The other thing, I never would have got into the police force. In the 1980s, when I joined the police, if I'd had a label like autism, there is no way they would have recruited me because the prejudice then was just so great. In society, it's constant the way that autism is associated with inability to do stuff. I think I've probably had a more successful career. Well, it's mixed, isn't it? I think I got a lot of jobs because they didn't know I was autistic, but then I didn't hold on to a lot of jobs because they didn't know I was autistic and I didn't know. You know what I mean? I think I might have had more longevity in jobs had it been known. Actually, my recent experience kind of disproves that because during the pandemic I had three jobs. One in a greengrocer, one in a factory, and then the school crossing patrol. And in all the three jobs, I hit problems. Knowing what I now know about being autistic and being openly autistic in saying "I am autistic and this is what it means" didn't protect me. It depends so much on whether other people really want to accommodate you or not, and I'm afraid in most situations, especially in those easy-come easy-go jobs, why would they? Why would they be bothered? Not when they can get somebody else who doesn't have that issue.

When I look at my CV, it's all like 12 months here, two years there, three years there, exceptionally four years somewhere. But some of that was maternity leave, so it doesn't really count. I haven't been able to, for whatever reason, a number of reasons, I haven't been able to sustain five, ten, 15, 20 years in a job. The good thing is that this is actually becoming less unusual these days. You know, people aren't doing 30 years for the same employer and leaving with a gold watch like they did when I was young. When I worked at a bookseller when I was young, I used to see these people having their leaving parties after 30 years, and I used to think, I just find it unimaginable. I mean it's funny really, because being autistic, people might suppose that I would crave routine and familiarity, which to some extent I do, but I need challenge, and I go into a job, and once I've kind of fixed whatever it is that needed fixing, as soon as it gets into just the maintenance and the running of the thing, I lose interest. I think if there is a common theme in all the work that I've done, it is problem-solving and intellectually stimulating but with a social purpose. I'm particularly motivated by wanting to make a difference to people who are disempowered.

More recently, my husband got seriously ill, and I had to abandon my career for a while so I did part-time work while I looked after him. When he recovered, we decided to move up from the south to the north of England, and moved to a much cheaper property and freed up some money so that the pressure was off him to have to work for a bit, and I went into working in libraries, prison libraries, doing the school crossing patrol. I got my autism diagnosis, finally, and now I'm kind of transitioning back into more of a kind of research career. So quite an amazingly varied career.

The biggest change post-diagnosis was reframing life events in a way that made various misunderstandings and mishaps seem much more understandable and much less my fault. That alone was huge. But in many ways, immediately after my assessment things got worse before they got better. That was because I went looking for help and support. The psychologist who assessed me was planning to run a group for late-diagnosed women, but the others didn't want to attend so it got cancelled. The post-diagnosis service commissioned locally was really poor – low-paid inexperienced staff who weren't equipped to work with people like me who'd experienced trauma. They offered a fixed number of sessions to address a specific issue like benefits or housing. That didn't work for me at all. My challenges were existential, and I wanted to meet other late-diagnosed people like me.

Luckily, I got in touch with an autistic-led project in a neighbouring city, and they took pity on me. Technically, I was out of area, but they let me attend a post-diagnosis group for several weeks where I met other people like me. We worked through a programme looking at relationships, executive function and sensory issues. The best bit of all was hearing about other people's lives and realising my struggles were typical of being autistic and genuine and real.

However, the overall lack of appropriate support was devastating, and I had suicidal thoughts. But when I approached the crisis service, I was told I didn't qualify as being in crisis. At this point, I came close to giving up.

I felt overwhelmed by the enormity of what I was trying to cope with and the lack of support. My husband
was overwhelmed too and was not able to support me.
I got discharged from the mental health service at the
start of the pandemic as it was doing more harm than
good, and I knew they'd be under enormous pressure.

The biggest shift happened when I watched a video
interview on Twitter with an autistic psychotherapist.
I knew instantly we'd get on, and I've been seeing them
for over a year now. I have to fund it myself, but it's
worth it. For the first time, I feel I have appropriate support. There is nothing available through local services
that matches this. I often think I've reached the end, but
then I'll be presented with an unexpected life challenge
and I am glad of the opportunity to work things through.

In the past, I have tried to suppress my emotional
volatility, because I suppose if you look at the thing I
was saying before about meltdowns, in an attempt to
keep my emotions in check, it probably ended up with
them being suppressed and then kind of exploding vol-
canically rather than me finding ways to release that
emotional tension. And I think this is the thing that
psychotherapy is helping me to realise, that actually
I can sense when I am getting stressed. Just like this
morning, I had a shower and it smelt of chemicals: chlo-
rine. Now I always know when that happens it means

I'm getting stressed, but then what to do about it? So it's just knowing myself better, in the same way that somebody might go and watch a weepy, tear-jerking film because they might find it hard to get that emotion out there, but they know that if they watch something really, really sad, they'll end up with a release. So I suppose there are ways of trying to do that, and I suppose in a way that's partly trying not to wear the mask of "I'm not feeling this emotion, I'm not acknowledging this emotion." And there's a reason why. There was a reason why we did all these things. I don't remember my early childhood as being particularly traumatic; it was very confusing, though. No doubt, I probably started doing these kind of compensations and things much earlier than I remember because I think so much of it is subliminal, isn't it? I think the thing about the diagnosis is you start consciously thinking about this stuff.

I would say that I have had regular burnouts throughout adult life, often work-related. Often something physical has happened that saved me. Just before my autism diagnosis, I had a twelve-and-a-half-year-old dog who I loved beyond description. I got this dog when I was breaking up from a very dysfunctional relationship, and I got him as a puppy because I knew that I would go back to this relationship. And I knew I mustn't. And I thought the only thing that I could think of was getting a dog for companionship and love, and someone to hold, and that would give me the strength to not go back to this relationship. This dog developed heart failure, so he collapsed and had to be resuscitated by the vet, and then we had another few months. We knew he was dying, and I was beside myself. One night, I came home from work and my husband said, "The vet said it's time; we have to let him go." And, of course, now I know I am autistic, I needed more processing time. I couldn't even speak. Not only that, but as we were going into the vet, the vet said to me, "Because his heart is so weak, I don't think it's going to be an easy death and I don't want you to be here." My husband was sobbing in the car park, he was distraught, so then I was torn between being with my dog or my husband who wasn't coping, so I ended up in the car park comforting my husband while my dog was dying. And then, of course, I go in and the vet said, "he passed peacefully." And I'm thinking, "Why wasn't I there?" It was awful.

After my dog died, I survived two weeks before adopting another dog. You know the thing where everybody says, "Oh, it's too soon, it is too soon." I adopted a six-year-old dog. It was like a miracle. We went to see a puppy, and the puppy kept biting my husband. It was just at the mouthing stage. I said to them, "Have you got an older dog because I think it might help my husband to see what this puppy is going to grow into?" And they brought through the most depressed dog I've ever seen. She was just, I can't describe it, you know when somebody just gives out an energy, just so sad. I got home and I couldn't get her out of my head. We decided not to adopt the puppy. We went away campervanning and we were so distraught we forgot to take any bedding with us. And when we came home and went back on to the website where the puppy was advertised, this sad dog, this six-year-old sad dog, was advertised for rehoming by the people. And I thought, goodness. So I rang them straight up and said I want to adopt her. And they said, "Well, are you sure?" I said yes. And we went straight over.

You know, she was terrified and sad. And she became the next love of my life, this beautiful dog. And then what happened was, because my old dog had had heart failure, I could barely walk him more than 100 metres before he was exhausted, so I hadn't been walking. And my new dog, she was so full of fear and nervous energy, and she didn't know what to do with herself, so I thought the only thing I can think of is taking her out into the countryside, away from everybody, and we'll just walk. Because border terriers, they love walking. They will walk all day. So we'd walk for miles and miles and miles. And then, of course, I didn't realise, but once we were coming back from a walk one day, I went to put one of my feet on the ground and I just couldn't put my foot down. I had given myself bursitis and tendinitis without realising, so I ended up immobilised.

Funnily enough, this is the burnout point: I needed to be immobilised. This helped me to realise that I really wasn't coping at work because of management. When my foot went and the physiotherapist said I'm going to sign you off work for six weeks, I wanted to hug and kiss her, because for me, it's only when I stop doing something that I realise how impossible it has been. When I was away from that job and away from the micromanaging and bullying, I thought I can't do it. I never went back to it. I was signed off sick from stress then, and I ended up leaving. So burnout to me is often complicated because it is a psychological thing, but it often has physical components in that when I'm in burnout I start over-exercising and then I'll damage myself. I don't know how recovered I am until I actually attempt to do it.

I suppose the thing that I feel most passionately about at the moment is the older, unrecognised autistic people. And my real concern is about them in residential care homes, in various kinds of settings. I am so worried about what's happening to them. This is affecting autistic people of all ages, but we know that the least diagnosed cohort of autistic people are those who are over 60. But they are still there. As you get older, a lot of your rights get eroded. So, the thing that is on my mind a lot, and it's not just because I'm getting older, it's about those people who didn't get the opportunity that I had. Thank goodness I found out when I did. I didn't want to go into old age not knowing. I did think I might have some kind of an unusual personality disorder or whatever, you know, but actually the answer was so plain and simple. Really plain and simple. And I just think it was that nobody ever actually put everything together. What I used to do when I worked with somebody as a social worker, I would do a timeline of their life and I would look at all the different strands of their life – what was happening, where they work, where they were living, who they were with – to try to make sense of it as a big picture with everything that was happening, taking the ecological approach. Whereas here, a lot of the time, it's just looking at the psychology of the individual rather than looking at everything else. It also goes the other way in that people were so keen to say it was nothing to do with my psychology; it was to do with this or that or the other. Actually, it was to do with my psychology – for want of a better word, my neurotype.

I am much happier when I don't compare myself to non-autistic people – my way of doing things is so different. Getting diagnosed and connecting with other autistic people has been a huge help in this respect. There's still a lot of stigma and misunderstanding in society in general, but there are some safe spaces now where I feel understood.

CHAPTER 9

Talking about the stories

IN THIS CHAPTER, we look at the topics that were evident in the stories of the participants in the book. The themes ranged from getting an autism diagnosis and sharing the diagnosis, to social experiences, masking and burnout. Each topic includes quotes from the participants. Some of these quotes may not have been in their chapter but were part of the original interviews. The idea of this chapter is to explore the similarities and differences for each of the participants.

Diagnosis of autism

For each individual, the journey to autism diagnosis had its own trajectory. Sydney said, "My journey to diagnosis began at age 36 when I finally had time to really put my mind to finding out what was going wrong in my life and why...I had such tremendous social problems."

The theme of life difficulties also resonated for Elizabeth who described her life as a "tragic-comedic train wreck" and explained that her request for assessment of autism was so that her children and grandchildren would have a greater understanding of themselves and their own autism diagnoses.

Reading or hearing about others' experiences of autism helped Zoë and Rebecca recognise their own autism. Zoë acknowledged that s'he might be autistic after reading "an article on the expression of autism in adult females... I was astounded. It was me. It was everything about me." Zoë hadn't been seeking the article; it was linked to their interest in wellness and health and the reading s'he did about that. For Rebecca, she recognised that she might be autistic partly due to autism awareness training through work: "Everything they said was really resonating and it was like a lightbulb moment for me." It was a gradual process for Rebecca, and the growing number of affirming resources about autism helped her to engage in an assessment of autism. Elizabeth was also helped by reading an article on experiences of autistic women. She said, "I started reading it, and hello."

Julian had an autism assessment at the prompting of her partner who had been reading about autism. This prompting was linked to the communication challenges that Julian and her partner were experiencing due to

Julian's alexithymia "which is where I really don't know what I'm feeling about things a lot of the time... That can be challenging in relationships if I don't know what I'm feeling about things." Although Matilda wasn't directly influenced by her life partner, she partnered with mental health professionals who recommended an autism assessment. Matilda said, "I did have a psychiatrist actually ask me, 'Has anyone ever suggested that you might be autistic?' I was just like, 'No, I can't deal with this conversation right now.'" It wasn't until Matilda had worked on her mental health that she was able to process the idea of being autistic.

Rose said about her autism journey that "the primary reason I have got assessed at the age of nearly 59 was because I didn't want to become my mother...and the other thing I thought about was my biggest dread of being parked in a residential care home for old people... So I thought my best chance of escaping that fate – those two fates really – was to get diagnosed and to see if I might be autistic and then to be able to say, 'I am autistic and I need X, Y, Z.'"

For each of the participants, the journey to diagnosis was a progressive one, where unexplained struggles, mental health conditions or life circumstances created an awareness of difference from their peers. For Elizabeth, Zoë and Rebecca, the catalyst was reading about or hearing others' experiences of autism diagnosis and the affinity that came from that.

The challenges of obtaining a diagnosis was discussed by the participants. Matilda spoke about the two-year wait for an assessment. She chose to go through the private system for an assessment to avoid the wait and instead "paid ridiculous sums of money". She acknowledged that "it's so hard getting a diagnosis if you can't pay for it". Elizabeth said, "There was no point at that stage in me going through the full diagnostic procedure as they were talking about $2000 or $3000 and I'm on the old age pension."

Julian also experienced challenges as her request for assessment was challenged by her doctor who said, "Why would you want to get diagnosed? You've got a good job, a good relationship, and you've managed up to this time." Similarly, the wait for the autism assessment was 12 months, and that was because she got in on the cancellation of someone else's appointment. Julian said, "It was a long process."

Although Zoë had "a professional, very, very thorough diagnosis", s'he felt the pain of not being believed by their friends. S'he said, "People are still going, 'I don't believe you'...which honestly put me into more isolation than I was before."

The cost of assessment and the assessment wait

times appeared to be an issue across multiple countries as the participants shared similar stories. The impact of the difficulties in accessing an autism diagnosis from a practitioner who understands the nuances of autism can mean that individuals with autism may not receive the understanding and support they need to navigate life and society. The delays in diagnosis, and particularly for the participants here who were diagnosed anywhere from their 30s to early 70s, meant that there is a lot more to unpack about the diagnosis and to find ways of safely unmasking and discovering their own community of support.

After receiving an autism diagnosis, the feelings from the participants were often positive and echoed feelings of relief as the diagnosis explained many things. Elizabeth said, "It was such a relief to finally have an explanation that actually fitted all of these stray bits and pieces." And Rebecca said, "I think...getting my diagnosis from the background of affirming literature and resources, it actually helped me to accept myself." Having the autism diagnosis explained one's self and this was framed as a positive aspect. Matilda used her autism diagnosis as permission to be herself and to "be okay with my sensory needs". This was important as, before, Matilda would refrain from using sensory tools such as sunglasses and comfortable clothing.

Rebecca discussed the need for processing time when receiving an autism diagnosis. She said, "I think when you get your official diagnosis, just give yourself six months to a year to process that. People process a lot of things leading up to the diagnosis, but then after the diagnosis there is a lot to unpack and process." Rose noted that this occurred for herself, where "the amazing thing about when you get your diagnosis is that you start tracking back and every day something comes to mind when I think, 'Oh, of course.' It's hard work because the older you are when you get your diagnosis, the more years of stuff you've got to track back through."

Sharing the diagnosis

Sharing the diagnosis with others comes with its own challenges and opportunities. Sydney said that she "tell[s] everybody in an effort to pre-excuse any social faux pas I might make". This pre-empting can act as a defence mechanism, particularly in light of the social difficulties that are faced throughout life. By pre-empting the difficulty, Sydney was able to set the tone for the conversation or social interaction. Elizabeth said that she shares her diagnosis: "My friends, colleagues, at the moment – I have come out to all of these people."

Rose was also open about her diagnosis. She said,

"I'm generally really open about being autistic – I mention it everywhere. It's surprising how often someone responds by saying someone close to them is autistic, or they think that they might be." Also, during the assessment process, Rose phoned her adult children and told them that she was being assessed for autism. This was a catalyst for conversations within the family about autism, and in providing support to her children and grandchild who were also autistic.

Rebecca was open about her autism at work, and built it in as a strength with the people that she worked with, and Matilda viewed sharing as advocacy. She said, "I think if we don't share the actual experience of what it's actually like being autistic, then people aren't going to know or have that understanding with their kids and themselves as well." Personally, though, Matilda took time to process her diagnosis before sharing it with family as she "knew that it would instigate some interesting conversations". She needed to be prepared in herself before sharing.

Julian was selective in sharing her diagnosis and hadn't shared her autism diagnosis at work as it was not relevant to the situation; however, friends knew and were "fine with that".

Zoë had shared their diagnosis with friends but found the process to be traumatising as s'he experienced negative feedback or disbelief. This significantly impacted their relationships when s'he was not believed. S'he said, "That was very traumatising for me because it meant that I really wasn't safe to share." Another reason that Zoë chooses not to share their diagnosis is that when s'he was diagnosed, Asperger's was still a diagnosis, but when the terminology was changed to autism, the idea of autism was perceived by others as "non-speaking and with other developmental disabilities...they are like, 'You are not autistic, you are not like my disabled nephew.' So that's challenging."

Overall, many of the participants received affirmation and acceptance when they shared about their diagnosis. The exception to this was Zoë who experienced disbelief from their friends. Feeling safe to share was key for Zoë, and also to a lesser extent for Julian who was more selective in who she shared her diagnosis with.

Social experiences

Each participant mentioned that making and maintaining friendships was difficult. Matilda said, "I find relationships quite difficult, and friendships." She was not alone in this, with Elizabeth having serial friends where "you have a friend for a while and then they disappear out of your life". Julian said that her teenage years were lonely and "it was noticeable that I didn't have friends for most of that time".

Difficulty making and maintaining friendships can start as a recognition of feeling different from peers, particularly as children. Sydney said that she was aware that she was different to others, even at a young age. Elizabeth noted this too, saying that "the kids already know that they are different and that they don't have any friends". Matilda said that she "never really fit. I was always the slightly weird one."

A limited number of friends was not a bad thing. Rebecca found that she would make a game of not speaking to anyone each day at university – and found the lack of social interaction "restful and refreshing". Elizabeth noted that she did not want to engage with people who were not interesting, that she was "looking for another group of people like me, but there weren't any". Julian had a similar social situation where "all the women were very much into their long hair and their fingernails and getting dressed up in fancy clothes and going out at night. I just don't fit in with that." The differences in interests meant that often it was not worth engaging with people who did not understand them or with whom they had nothing in common.

At times, social isolation occurred through bullying

and ostracism. Sydney said that she struggled with "all kinds of relationships, just not understanding what I was doing wrong. Friends would just stop being friends with no explanation and often with a lot of hostility."

Five of the seven participants in this book experienced bullying by peers. For some, it was verbal threats or abuse. Julian said that she was called "weird freak", and Rebecca experienced verbal insults too. Rebecca also experienced physical bullying where she had her lunch stolen, lunch money taken and was threatened with physical harm.

Bullying didn't always end with the completion of schooling. Both Rose and Rebecca were bullied in the workplace for abiding by the rules. Rose said that her problems at work centred around "some kind of dishonesty, bullying or abuse". It didn't need to be specifically targeted at her, but it did affect her deeply. When asked by her family if she could just ignore it, she said, "No, I couldn't." This sense of justice and abiding by the rules was similar for Rebecca who said that she experienced bullying in the workplace because she did not accept the unprofessional behaviour of her colleagues. As a result of speaking out, she was bullied by these colleagues.

While not experiencing bullying as such, Matilda did experience negativity from her work management as she would have "quite a lot of run-ins with my managers who would want me to do things that I wouldn't do because I wasn't comfortable with treating my team in that way".

Post-diagnosis, Julian found that she had more friends because she was able to connect with like-minded people. Julian joined a theatre group for autistic people – a place where she felt that she fit in. Sydney also found that when she married, she gained her partner's friends. Rebecca made people and psychology a special interest so that she could understand social dynamics and said that "the first actual real friendship that I made was in my first job out of uni" with a person who had an autistic family member and understood neurodiversity. This friendship has been a long-term friendship and has led to other friendships.

Zoë, however, found that, post-diagnosis, their social connections were obliterated. S'he said, "I was so excited to learn about [autism], but really, it has turned my life upside down and not for the best. I lost my friends [and] my marriage fell apart." The repercussions of the diagnosis meant that Zoë didn't have a social network to support them.

Masking

Masking – or camouflaging – is the minimising of or hiding autistic traits[28] to fit in socially, or, at the minimum, to avoid ostracism or bullying. Masking is often a coping strategy and can help the autistic individual form social connections, and to gain and maintain employment.[29]

However, masking can contribute to a delay in getting an autism diagnosis[30] and can be detrimental to the mental health and wellbeing of the autistic individual due to the suppression of their authentic self.[31]

Most participants in this book recognised that they engaged in masking. For some, it was more often than others. Sydney said that she masks "every time I go out, every time I have to speak to someone. Times when I haven't masked are noteworthy." Matilda said that masking for her was "pushing myself into social situations, trying to be a normal person". Matilda also recognised the benefits of masking, saying that it was "kind of useful, being able to walk into a different situation and be someone who fits in there, but it's exhausting if you are doing it all the time and you don't recognise what you are doing". After her diagnosis of autism, Matilda recognised the level of masking that was going on and gave herself permission to "unmask" at times and to not do as many social activities.

Rose found the concept of masking to be confusing. She questioned whether it meant that she was not being authentic, and what the repercussions were from that. "I think I had this notion that I was like this Russian doll with all the layers and layers, and I was going to get into the middle and find that there was nothing there. That it was a series of masks." Rose preferred the word "camouflage" instead of "masking" as it better described the act of trying to fit in and not be bullied. Masking, or fitting in, for Rose centred on her appearance – "in other words, how I dressed". The style of clothing would change depending on the employment role, or the perceived social requirement.

Julian noted that she didn't mask and associated that with growing up in a family where autistic traits were normalised.

For Rebecca, masking was something that developed as she grew older and became more socially aware. She said, "I don't think I really had much awareness of how I appeared to other people in primary school. And then it was more in high school that I started noticing, getting negative feedback from others in terms of how I would appear or present to people or interact with them." Masking was a tool to gain and maintain social interactions and friendships. Rebecca credited her ability to mask in helping her to "get further in the workplace than if I didn't or couldn't mask". Rebecca recognised that "masking definitely has served me well, but I think it has come at a cost. It is exhausting and I've been going through the process of my own diagnosis of looking at how much do I unmask versus do I show my authentic self, and then how much is that actually going to cost me in terms of my work and my income and friendships and thing, like that. To me personally, I think it's a bit of a compromise."

Burnout

Autistic burnout has been described as excessive fatigue, high levels of stress and a reduced capacity to manage social interactions, sensory situations and general life skills.[32] Matilda thought that masking and burnout were linked. She said, "I think often the pressure that we feel to do things in an acceptable way to meet other people's standards and to work in a way that doesn't work for us because we are trying to mask, because we are trying to fit in, is often what results in a burnout."

Julian said that she had "been on the edge of burnout a few times"; however, being self-employed and creating strategies to recover allowed her to avoid the full impact of burnout.

Rebecca experienced burnout through a combination of study, relationships and working. The combination exceeded her capacity. The burnout contributed to the onset of chronic health conditions which have impacted her ongoing ability to work full-time. Rebecca said, "Potentially, my health may have not been as badly affected by pushing myself and then getting burnt out. Maybe I wouldn't have had such bad health challenges as I have now that still affect me."

Rose, when exceeding her limitations and becoming burnt out, would experience physical symptoms. The pressure of studying for exams as a child led to four weeks in bed due to a back injury. The result of a toxic work environment led to physical overexertion as a coping strategy – resulting in six weeks off work. Both of these enforced rest periods allowed Rose time to recover, and to reassess priorities and workloads.

Zoë, at the time of the interviews, was experiencing significant burnout due to work, saying, "I've needed an assistant or a team [at work] for a long time and they haven't been willing to give me one. I'm just so burnt out. So burnt out." Zoë's work was physically and emotionally demanding, and combined with a relationship breakdown, s'he recognised that it has been "a hell of a year...it's too much". Zoë also linked masking with burnout and said, "I certainly recognise the exhaustion, the inability to discuss what you are actually going through with anyone because they are not going to believe you. People see you are doing so well, so you are fine. I don't even know how to unmask. I don't. Because when I do,

I lose relationships." That precarity led Zoë to feelings of exhaustion and hopelessness.

Burnout also led to mental health issues for Matilda. Matilda said, "I think my psychosis comes from an autistic burnout." The effects for Matilda were the euphoria that came from psychosis, and, later, setting strict limitations on her activities to prevent future burnout.

Similarly, Elizabeth experienced mental health concerns due to burnout; however, burnout was framed as a nervous breakdown at the time. These breakdowns were precipitated by difficulties in relationships, by a tumultuous work environment and by a significant house move. The effects of burnout for Elizabeth were depression, anxiety and suicidal ideation.

The research literature recognises that more research needs to be done to understand autistic burnout from the lived experience of autistic people.[33] As noted by the participants in this book, autistic burnout can affect mental health, general functioning and overall wellbeing. Participants showed that they understood the cause of burnout for themselves and were able to put strategies in place. For example, Julian was self-employed and was able to set boundaries for what worked for her, and Matilda was very clear that she would only work part-time as she knew that she needed time away from work to manage her health.

Intelligence

An interesting phenomenon within this book is that each participant had high academic ability. This could be due to the small sample size and the method of recruiting participants; however, it is interesting that each participant had a late diagnosis and some mentioned that their academic ability at school may have caused some of their autistic traits to have been missed by educators. It would be beneficial to explore whether high levels of intelligence contribute to a later diagnosis of autism due to the cognitive strengths of the individual enabling them to mask their autistic traits in order to fit in with their peers. This level of masking ties in with studies of twice exceptionality which is the combination of giftedness (high ability) and disability. While this topic is outside of the scope of this book, there is much research in this area.

About her time at school, Elizabeth said, "I was academically able too so that covered up a whole lot of other things." Similarly, Julian said, "I think because I was clever and I always did well at school and that's all they thought about at that time...anything else didn't get picked up."

Rose recognised that her academic ability has helped her. She said, "I had an IQ that was way up there, so I

was like, 'I don't have any cognitive issues, you know.'
I was hyperlexic as a child, I was ahead on all my milestones, I was never behind on any developmental milestones." Rebecca also recognised that "the high IQ helps,
it has helped me a lot". And Matilda spoke about how
her special interests "tend to be very academic and
brain and intellectual and thinking heavy", which also
helped with her academic studies and work.

Zoë said, "I am just sub-genius. Apparently, my IQ is
129, and I need a 130 to be a genius, so I am sub-genius."
However, Zoë didn't think that this level of intelligence
helped them because their friends wouldn't believe that
s'he was autistic. S'he said, "It meant that I wasn't going
to be believed because my intelligence is high enough
that I effectively pulled the wool over my own eyes in
addition to other people's eyes for a long time." Before
their diagnosis, Zoë had used their intelligence to pick
up on social cues and adjust their presentation of self
to avoid ostracism.

The breadth of the spectrum

The participants in this book are of varying ages and
have had late diagnoses of autism. Late diagnosis has
been partially attributed to a lack of awareness of the
breadth of the autism spectrum in previous decades.

Matilda said, "I grew up in the 1980s, and, of course, that was a whole different world in terms of understanding autism…it wasn't really a thing when I was a kid." Elizabeth, who was diagnosed autistic toward her 70s, noted that she would not have been recognised as autistic as a child, and even if she had been, "How much support and knowledge were there in a country town in the 1950s, 1960s and 1970s?" Similarly, Rose recognised that there would not have been awareness and support if she had been diagnosed when she was a child in the 1970s, saying that having a diagnosis then would not have helped at all.

The effects of diversity

Recognising the breadth of the spectrum has been a key theme in this book about the journeys of females with a late diagnosis of autism. The idea was to bring together stories from a range of women across different ages to show the many ways that autism is represented in this cohort. In showing a greater breadth of the spectrum, it is hoped that the stories resonate and provide a sense of belonging and community for the reader.

Additionally, when autism is recognised in its various presentations, it may increase the recognition of autism in the community and allow for accommodations in the workplace, social situations and throughout the ageing process. It is hoped that by sharing stories we can help those who are coming after us.

For me, the stories shared by the participants have had an impact. I find myself in little pieces of each, and the insights have explained some things that I would not have worked out myself. For example, when Rebecca said that during burnout she could only eat bland foods because of sensory overwhelm, that resonated with me and explained why I had done the same. Or when Matilda explained how vigilant she was about only taking on a small number of activities at a time, that gave me permission to do the same for myself, to look after myself in this way. Each participant has added greater meaning to my journey, and I hope that you have experienced the same.

In the next, and final, chapter of this book, a variety of resources are listed to provide further support and information about autism and the journey to diagnosis and beyond. These have been gathered from the participants as resources that have been useful to them.

CHAPTER 10

Final thoughts and resources

THE BENEFITS OF receiving an autism diagnosis – even a late diagnosis – have been undeniable for me. It has given me permission to find my own way in looking after myself and to embrace my own personality and quirks. However, in moments of overwhelm, there are times where I wish I wasn't the way that I am. I'll wish that there was a way that I could manage "normal" things. Like having friends visit for supper or negotiating shopping centres. Or even managing to work in an office like regular people do. But after recovering from the overwhelm – usually sensory or fatigue related – I'm able to counter that with self-compassion. I can be myself and that's okay.

The benefits of receiving an autism diagnosis for each participant varied, but overall it brought a greater understanding and acceptance of self. With this in mind, and to help others with their understanding of autism, each participant was asked what they wished others knew about autism. Their responses are included below.

What I wish others knew about autism

Sydney said, "I think one of the least-known things about autism is that we are more sensitive to all stimuli, and that seems to include sensitivity to medications (for me, anyway). On the rare occasions I seek medical help, I am almost always overdosed because I am given a full adult dose. Doctors *will not* accept that I need a lesser dosage and brush me off when I protest."

Matilda said, "I think a lot of autistic people have overwhelming empathy and I know I do. So things like, we can't read stuff where people get told off. Or watch things. I had never been able to watch slapstick with people getting hurt because I am like, 'Why is that funny? I don't understand, that person is hurt. Why are you laughing at them? That's really horrible.' And I think that can actually be really overwhelming, that feeling of being upset when you feel for that person – you really kind of feel that person's pain. And I think that's quite common in a lot of autistic people. But you maybe don't present it in the same way and people think because you don't present it in a certain way, then you don't feel it."

Elizabeth said, "I wish people would figure out the distinction between a spectrum and a continuum."

Julian said, "It can be so different for different people. I met a lot of different autistic people who I actually feel I have nothing in common with. There are a lot of autistic people who are into sci-fi and *Doctor Who* and all that sort of thing. That doesn't interest me in the slightest."

Rose said she wished people knew "how different the lived experience of being autistic is from the autism stereotypes most people base their knowledge on. Also, I wish people knew how being autistic affects every aspect of life from when we are born until we die and how rare it is for autism to have been taken into account when services are being designed."

Zoë said, "I would like the reader to know that autism looks different from how most people think it does, and it absolutely looks different in women and girls, especially older individuals, much older, who have learned to cope and mask for decades even. I would like them to understand that autism is a series of anomalies in neurological processing. It is not deficits. Sometimes it is strength, sometimes it is deficits. It is a sequence of anomalies."

Rebecca said, "I think the main struggle is just other people not understanding what autism actually is and having very outdated information about it and misconceptions about it. And also not really recognising what it looks like in different presentations. So not really recognising what it looks like in women, what does it look like in people who are not white, Caucasians. I think too, if you see a child struggling, it's always better to get them diagnosed and actually get them help and support from a young age because you may be able to prevent them from reaching burnout."

Lived experience

Listening to the voice of lived experience is essential to understanding autism from the perspective of autistic people. It is hoped, by sharing in the journeys to late diagnosis of the participants in this book, that you, the reader, have found new insights and have recognised yourself or a loved one in these stories. Thanks again to the participants who shared their stories of richness and depth in their personal journeys. It is hoped that these stories will contribute to the ripple effect and bring about a greater understanding of autism in its full spectrum.

Resources

A list of resources has been compiled, highlighting what has been useful to the book participants and would likely be useful to others. It is not a comprehensive list, but it is a starting point for future learning. These resources include books, podcasts, websites, blogs and research literature. These are intended to support you or others in the journey to diagnosis of autism and beyond.

Website resources

Chloé Hayden
www.chloehayden.com.au

I Can Network
https://icannetwork.online

Kristen Neff – Self-Compassion
https://self-compassion.org

National Autistic Society – Autistic fatigue and burnout
www.autism.org.uk/advice-and-guidance/topics/mental-health/autistic-fatigue/professionals

Reframing Autism – Celebrating and nurturing autistic identity
https://reframingautism.org.au

Spectrum Women
www.spectrumwomen.com

Summer Farrelly – Autistic Perspectives
https://summerfarrelly.com.au

Temple Grandin
www.templegrandin.com

Tony Attwood
https://tonyattwood.com.au

Yellow Ladybugs
www.yellowladybugs.com.au

Books

Sarah Bargiela and Sophie Standing. *Camouflage: The Hidden Lives of Autistic Women*. Jessica Kingsley Publishers, 2019.

Clem Bastow. *Late Bloomer: How an Autism Diagnosis Changed My Life*. Hardie Grant Books, 2021.

Hannah Louise Belcher. *Taking off the Mask: Practical Exercises to Help Understand and Minimise the Effects of Autistic Camouflaging*. Jessica Kingsley Publishers, 2022.

Barb Cook and Michelle Garnett (eds). *Spectrum*

Women: Walking to the Beat of Autism. Jessica Kingsley Publishers, 2018.

Barb Cook and Yenn Purkis. *The Autism and Neurodiversity Self-Advocacy Handbook: Developing the Skills to Determine Your Own Future*. Jessica Kingsley Publishers, 2022.

Hannah Gadsby. *Ten Steps to Nanette*. Allen & Unwin, 2022.

Francesca Happé, Rebecca Wood, Laura Crane, Alan Morrison and Ruth Moyse (eds). *Learning From Autistic Teachers*. Jessica Kingsley Publishers, 2022.

Rachael Lee Harris. *My Autistic Awakening: Unlocking the Potential for a Life Well Lived*. Rowman & Littlefield Publishers, 2015.

Laura James. *Odd Girl Out: An Autistic Woman in a Neurotypical World*. Bluebird Books for Life, 2017.

Renata Jurkevythz, Maura Campbell, Lisa Morgan and Barb Cook. *Spectrum Women: Autism and Parenting*. Jessica Kingsley Publishers, 2020.

Sandhya Menon, Donita Richards and Kushla Ross. *The Brain Forest*. Onwards and Upwards Psychology, 2022.

Jenara Nerenberg. *Divergent Mind: Thriving in a World That Wasn't Designed for You.* HarperCollins US, 2020.

Devon Price. *Unmasking Autism: The Power of Embracing Our Hidden Neurodiversity.* Monoray, 2022.

Steve Silberman. *NeuroTribes: The Legacy of Autism and How to Think Smarter About People Who Think Differently.* Allen & Unwin, 2015.

Emma Watts. *But You Said...?! A Story of Confusion Caused by Growing Up as an Undiagnosed Autistic Person.* Independently published, 2020.

Sonny Jane Wise. *The Neurodivergent Friendly Workbook of DBT Skills.* Independently published, 2022.

Resources for Australian First Nations people

Autism Aboriginal Way
www.facebook.com/groups/1478863162159107

Positive Partnerships – Resources for Aboriginal and Torres Strait Islander Peoples
www.positivepartnerships.com.au/resources/aboriginal-and-torres-strait-islander-peoples

Blogs

Actually Autistic – Non-speaking Autistic bloggers
https://wordpress.com/read/feeds/30372593/posts/
4191110340

Actually Autistic – What are your favourite Autistic blogs?
https://wordpress.com/read/feeds/30372593/posts/
4082949978

JKP Blog – Masking and Learning Self-Compassion
https://blog.jkp.com/2022/09/masking-and-learning-self-compassion

Podcasts

Squarepeg podcast
https://squarepeg.community/podcast

The Neurodivergent Woman Podcast by Monique Mitchelson and Dr Michelle Livock
www.ndwomanpod.com

The Yellow Ladybugs Podcast
https://podcasts.apple.com/au/podcast/the-yellow-ladybugs-podcast/id1611515609

Academic research

Bargiela, S., Steward, R., & Mandy, W. (2016). The experiences of late-diagnosed women with autism spectrum conditions: An investigation of the female autism phenotype. *Journal of Autism and Developmental Disorders*, *46*(10), 3281–3294. https://doi.org/http://dx.doi.org/10.1007/s10803-016-2872-8

Cage, E., & Troxell-Whitman, Z. (2019). Understanding the reasons, contexts and costs of camouflaging for autistic adults. *Journal of Autism and Developmental Disorders*, *49*(5), 1899–1911. https://doi.org/http://dx.doi.org/10.1007/s10803-018-03878-x

Hull, L., Petrides, K. V., Allison, C., Smith, P., Baron-Cohen, S., Lai, M.-C., & Mandy, W. (2017). "Putting on my best normal": Social camouflaging in adults with autism spectrum conditions. *Journal of Autism and Developmental Disorders*, *47*(8), 2519–2534. https://doi.org/http://dx.doi.org/10.1007/s10803-017-3166-5

Leedham, A., Thompson, A. R., Smith, R., & Freeth, M. (2019). "I was exhausted trying to figure it out": The experiences of females receiving an autism diagnosis in middle to late adulthood. *Autism*, *24*(1), 135–146. https://doi.org/10.1177/1362361319853442

Murphy, S., Flower, R., & Jellett, R. (2022). Women seeking an autism diagnosis in Australia: A qualitative exploration of factors that help and hinder. *Autism*, *27*(3), 1–14. https://doi.org/10.1177/13623613221117911

Raymaker, D., Teo, A., Steckler, N., Lentz, B., Scharer, M., Delos Santos, A., Kapp, S., Hunter, M., Joyce, A., & Nicolaidis, C. (2020). "Having all of your internal resources exhausted beyond measure and being left with no clean-up crew": Defining autistic burnout. *Autism in Adulthood*, *2*(2), 132–143. www.liebertpub.com/doi/epdf/10.1089/aut.2019.0079

Seers, K., & Hogg, R. C. (2021). "You don't look autistic": A qualitative exploration of women's experiences of being the "autistic other". *Autism*, *25*(6), 1553–1564. https://doi.org/10.1177/1362361321993722

Endnotes

Glossary

1   APA. (2022). *Diagnostic and Statistical Manual of Mental Disorders*: DSM-5-TR (5th ed., text revision). American Psychiatric Association Publishing.

2   Raymaker, D., Teo, A., Steckler, N., Lentz, B., Scharer, M., Delos Santos, A., Kapp, S., Hunter, M., Joyce, A., & Nicolaidis, C. (2020). "Having all of your internal resources exhausted beyond measure and being left with no clean-up crew": Defining autistic burnout. *Autism in Adulthood*, *2*(2), 132–143. www.liebertpub.com/doi/epdf/10.1089/aut.2019.0079

3   McQuaid, G. A., Lee, N. R., & Wallace, G. L. (2021). Camouflaging in autism spectrum disorder: Examining the roles of sex, gender identity, and diagnostic timing. *Autism*, 13623613211042131. https://doi.org/10.1177/13623613211042131

4   Cleveland Clinic. (2022). Neurodivergent. https://my.clevelandclinic.org/health/symptoms/23154-neurodivergent

5   Milner, V., McIntosh, H., Colvert, E., & Happé, F. (2019). A qualitative exploration of the female experience of autism spectrum disorder (ASD). *Journal of Autism and Developmental Disorders*, *49*(6), 2389–2402. https://doi.org/http://dx.doi.org/10.1007/s10803-019-03906-4

6   Kapp, S. K., Steward, R., Crane, L., Elliott, D., Elphick, C., Pellicano, E., & Russell, G. (2019). "People should be allowed to do what they like": Autistic adults' views and experiences of stimming. *Autism*, *23*(7), 1782–1792. https://doi.org/10.1177/1362361319829628

Chapter 1

7   Allely, C. S. (2019). Understanding and recognising the female phenotype of autism spectrum disorder and the "camouflage" hypothesis: A systematic PRISMA review. *Advances in Autism*, *5*(1), 14–37. https://doi.org/http://dx.doi.org/10.1108/AIA-09-2018-0036

8   Allely, C. S. (2019). Understanding and recognising the female phenotype of autism spectrum disorder and the "camouflage" hypothesis: A systematic PRISMA review. *Advances in Autism*, *5*(1), 14–37. https://doi.org/http://dx.doi.org/10.1108/AIA-09-2018-0036

9   Bargiela, S., Steward, R., & Mandy, W. (2016). The experiences of late-diagnosed women with autism spectrum conditions: An investigation of the female autism phenotype. *Journal of Autism and Developmental Disorders*, *46*(10), 3281–3294. https://doi.org/http://dx.doi.org/10.1007/s10803-016-2872-8

10   Bargiela, S., Steward, R., & Mandy, W. (2016). The experiences of late-diagnosed women with autism spectrum conditions: An investigation of the female autism phenotype. *Journal of Autism and Developmental Disorders*, *46*(10), 3281–3294. https://doi.org/http://dx.doi.org/10.1007/s10803-016-2872-8

11   Allely, C. S. (2019). Understanding and recognising the female phenotype of autism spectrum disorder and the "camouflage" hypothesis: A systematic PRISMA review. *Advances in Autism*, *5*(1), 14–37. https://doi.org/http://dx.doi.org/10.1108/AIA-09-2018-0036

12   Allely, C. S. (2019). Understanding and recognising the female phenotype of autism spectrum disorder and the "camouflage" hypothesis: A systematic PRISMA review. *Advances in Autism*, *5*(1), 14–37. https://doi.org/http://dx.doi.org/10.1108/AIA-09-2018-0036

13   Leedham, A., Thompson, A. R., Smith, R., & Freeth, M. (2019). "I was exhausted trying to figure it out": The experiences of females receiving an autism diagnosis in middle to late adulthood. *Autism*, *24*(1), 135–146.

Lilley, R., Lawson, W., Hall, G., Mahony, J., Clapham, H., Heyworth, M., Arnold, S. R. C., Trollor, J. N., Yudell, M., & Pellicano, E. (2021). "A way to be me": Autobiographical reflections of autistic adults diagnosed in mid-to-late adulthood. *Autism*, 13623613211050694. https://doi.org/10.1177/13623613211050694

14   Pellicano, E., Lawson, W., Hall, G., Mahony, J., Lilley, R., Arnold, S., Trollor, J., & Yudell, M. (2020). Uncovering the hidden histories of late-diagnosed autistic adults. Autism CRC Knowledge Centre. www.autismcrc.

com.au/knowledge-centre/reports/uncovering-hidden-histories-late-diagnosed-autistic-adults

15   Eya-Mist, R., Jensen, K., Kamilla Woznica, M., & Mottron, L. (2021). Childhood diagnoses in individuals identified as autistics in adulthood. *Molecular Autism*, *12*, 1–7. https://doi.org/http://dx.doi.org/10.1186/s13229-021-00478-y

Gesi, C., Migliarese, G., Torriero, S., Capellazzi, M., Omboni, A. C., Cerveri, G., & Mencacci, C. (2021). Gender differences in misdiagnosis and delayed diagnosis among adults with autism spectrum disorder with no language or intellectual disability. *Brain Sciences*, *11*(7), 912. https://doi.org/http://dx.doi.org/10.3390/brainsci11070912

16   Eya-Mist, R., Jensen, K., Kamilla Woznica, M., & Mottron, L. (2021). Childhood diagnoses in individuals identified as autistics in adulthood. *Molecular Autism*, *12*, 1–7. https://doi.org/http://dx.doi.org/10.1186/s13229-021-00478-y

17   Gesi, C., Migliarese, G., Torriero, S., Capellazzi, M., Omboni, A. C., Cerveri, G., & Mencacci, C. (2021). Gender differences in misdiagnosis and delayed diagnosis among adults with autism spectrum disorder with no language or intellectual disability. *Brain Sciences*, *11*(7), 912. https://doi.org/http://dx.doi.org/10.3390/brainsci11070912

18   Geurts, H. M., & Jansen, M. D. (2011). A retrospective chart study: The pathway to a diagnosis for adults referred for ASD assessment. *Autism*, *16*(3), 299–305. https://doi.org/10.1177/1362361311421775

19   Bargiela, S., Steward, R., & Mandy, W. (2016). The experiences of late-diagnosed women with autism spectrum conditions: An investigation of the female autism phenotype. *Journal of Autism and Developmental Disorders*, *46*(10), 3281–3294. https://doi.org/http://dx.doi.org/10.1007/s10803-016-2872-8

20   Gesi, C., Migliarese, G., Torriero, S., Capellazzi, M., Omboni, A. C., Cerveri, G., & Mencacci, C. (2021). Gender differences in misdiagnosis and delayed diagnosis among adults with autism spectrum disorder with no language or intellectual disability. *Brain Sciences*, *11*(7), 912. https://doi.org/http://dx.doi.org/10.3390/brainsci11070912

21   Clarke, E., Hull, L., Loomes, R., McCormick, C. E. B., Sheinkopf, S. J., & Mandy, W. (2021). Assessing gender differences in autism spectrum disorder using the Gendered Autism Behavioral Scale (GABS): An exploratory study. *Research in Autism Spectrum Disorders*, *88*, 101844.

Eya-Mist, R., Jensen, K., Kamilla Woznica, M., & Mottron, L. (2021). Childhood diagnoses in individuals identified as autistics in adulthood.

Molecular Autism, 12, 1–7. https://doi.org/http://dx.doi.org/10.1186/s13229-021-00478-y

22   Clarke, E., Hull, L., Loomes, R., McCormick, C. E. B., Sheinkopf, S. J., & Mandy, W. (2021). Assessing gender differences in autism spectrum disorder using the Gendered Autism Behavioral Scale (GABS): An exploratory study. *Research in Autism Spectrum Disorders, 88*, 101844.

Hull, L., Petrides, K. V., Allison, C., Smith, P., Baron-Cohen, S., Lai, M.-C., & Mandy, W. (2017). "Putting on my best normal": Social camouflaging in adults with autism spectrum conditions. *Journal of Autism and Developmental Disorders, 47*(8), 2519–2534. https://doi.org/http://dx.doi.org/10.1007/s10803-017-3166-5

23   Gesi, C., Migliarese, G., Torriero, S., Capellazzi, M., Omboni, A. C., Cerveri, G., & Mencacci, C. (2021). Gender differences in misdiagnosis and delayed diagnosis among adults with autism spectrum disorder with no language or intellectual disability. *Brain Sciences, 11*(7), 912. https://doi.org/http://dx.doi.org/10.3390/brainsci11070912

24   Leedham, A., Thompson, A. R., Smith, R., & Freeth, M. (2019). "I was exhausted trying to figure it out": The experiences of females receiving an autism diagnosis in middle to late adulthood. *Autism, 24*(1), 135–146.

McQuaid, G. A., Lee, N. R., & Wallace, G. L. (2021). Camouflaging in autism spectrum disorder: Examining the roles of sex, gender identity, and diagnostic timing. *Autism*, 13623613211042131. https://doi.org/10.1177/13623613211042131

25   Lewis, L. F. (2017). "We will never be normal": The experience of discovering a partner has autism spectrum disorder. *Journal of Marital and Family Therapy, 43*(4), 631–643. https://doi.org/http://dx.doi.org/10.1111/jmft.12231

26   Creswell, J. (2013). *Qualitative Inquiry and Research Design: Choosing Among Five Approaches* (3rd ed.). Sage.

27   Camm-Crosbie, L., Bradley, L., Shaw, R., Baron-Cohen, S., & Cassidy, S. (2018). "People like me don't get support": Autistic adults' experiences of support and treatment for mental health difficulties, self-injury and suicidality. *Autism, 23*(6), 1431–1441. https://doi.org/10.1177/1362361318816053

Chapter 9
28   Costley, D., Emerson, A., Ropar, D., & Sheppard, E. (2021). The anxiety caused by secondary schools for autistic adolescents: In their own words. *Education Sciences, 11*(11), 726. https://doi.org/http://dx.doi.org/10.3390/educsci11110726

29   Cage, E., & Troxell-Whitman, Z. (2019). Understanding the reasons, contexts and costs of camouflaging for autistic adults. *Journal of Autism and Developmental Disorders*, *49*(5), 1899–1911. https://doi.org/http://dx.doi.org/10.1007/s10803-018-03878-x

30   Cridland, E. K., Jones, S. C., Caputi, P., & Magee, C. A. (2014). Being a girl in a boys' world: Investigating the experiences of girls with autism spectrum disorders during adolescence. *Journal of Autism and Developmental Disorders*, *44*(6), 1261–1274. https://doi.org/http://dx.doi.org/10.1007/s10803-013-1985-6

31   Lilley, R., Lawson, W., Hall, G., Mahony, J., Clapham, H., Heyworth, M., Arnold, S. R. C., Trollor, J. N., Yudell, M., & Pellicano, E. (2021). "A way to be me": Autobiographical reflections of autistic adults diagnosed in mid-to-late adulthood. *Autism*, 13623613211050694. https://doi.org/10.1177/13623613211050694

32   Raymaker, D., Teo, A., Steckler, N., Lentz, B., Scharer, M., Delos Santos, A., Kapp, S., Hunter, M., Joyce, A., & Nicolaidis, C. (2020). "Having all of your internal resources exhausted beyond measure and being left with no clean-up crew": Defining autistic burnout. *Autism in Adulthood*, *2*(2), 132–143. www.liebertpub.com/doi/epdf/10.1089/aut.2019.0079

33   National Autistic Society. (2020). Autistic fatigue and burnout. www.autism.org.uk/advice-and-guidance/topics/mental-health/autistic-fatigue/professionals

Raymaker, D., Teo, A., Steckler, N., Lentz, B., Scharer, M., Delos Santos, A., Kapp, S., Hunter, M., Joyce, A., & Nicolaidis, C. (2020). "Having all of your internal resources exhausted beyond measure and being left with no clean-up crew": Defining autistic burnout. *Autism in Adulthood*, *2*(2), 132–143. www.liebertpub.com/doi/epdf/10.1089/aut.2019.0079